ETHNOGRAPHIC EYES

ETHNOGRAPHIC EYES

A Teacher's Guide to Classroom Observation

CAROLYN FRANK

Foreword by
Judith L. Green & Carol N. Dixon

HEINEMANN
Portsmouth, NH

Heinemann

361 Hanover Street
Portsmouth, NH 03801–3912
www.heinemann.com

Offices and agents throughout the world

Figure 2–1 from "Multiple Perspectives: Issues and Directions" by J. L. Green. In *Multidisciplinary Perspectives on Literacy Research* edited by R. Beach, J. L. Green, M. L. Kamil, and T. Shanahan. Copyright © 1992 by the National Council of Teachers of English. Reprinted by permission.

Figure 3–2 from *Participant Observation* by James P. Spradley. Copyright © 1980 by Holt, Rinehart and Winston. Adapted by permission of the publisher.

Library of Congress Cataloging-in-Publication Data
Frank, Carolyn.
    Ethnographic eyes : a teacher's guide to classroom observation / Carolyn Frank ; foreword by Judith L. Green and Carol N. Dixon ; [editor, Lois Bridges].
      p. cm.
    Includes bibliographical references and index.
    ISBN 0-325-00201-0 (alk. paper)
      1. Observation (Educational method). 2. Teaching—Social aspects—United States.
3. Classroom management—United States. 4. Teachers—Training of—United States.
I. Bird, Lois Bridges. II. Title.
LB1027.28.F73 1999
371.39—dc21   99-33452
                                                           CIP

Editor: Lois Bridges
Production: Denise Botelho/Colophon
Cover design: Darci Mehall/Aureo Design
Manufacturing: Louise Richardson

Printed in the United States of America on acid-free paper
10 09 08   VP   12 13 14

*This book is dedicated to Carol Dixon,
my friend and guide,
who reminds me that there is not just one way
but many ways.*

Contents

Foreword

JUDITH L. GREEN AND CAROL N. DIXON
Graduate School of Education
University of California, Santa Barbara

Observing is one of the most basic of human activities. Literally from the moment of birth, we observe in order to learn and to participate in our world. The ordinariness of observing is both its power and the reason that it is problematic. In everyday life, we seldom think about what guides our observations. We observe so that we can navigate a street, participate in a conversation, read a sign or traffic light, purchase a new outfit or enjoy a sunset. In such situations, there is an invisibility of the lens through which we observe. This invisibility results from the fact that unless something goes astray, we do not consciously think about the process of observing. Rather, we observe to accomplish other tasks, and the process is secondary to our purpose.

This form of observing leaves unexamined the ways in which our individual lenses influence what we see, what we interpret, what we come to understand, and how our observations may differ from those of others. These lenses can be thought of as formed by the past experiences we have had in similar situations, the values we hold for what should occur, our practical and educational training in different forms of observing, the purposes we have for observing in a particular context, and our awareness, or lack of awareness, of the ways in which differences in observations have consequences for others as well as for ourselves. For example, everyone who has gone to school assumes that they know what is expected of students, or what it means to be a student or a teacher. Parents or student teachers entering a classroom may assume that reading in this classroom is the same as it was when they were students—that only the books have changed. They hear the words, reading group, or even the name of a group (e.g., Panthers) and assume that it means the same that it did when they were in school. Their lenses lead them to particular expectations for what will occur next. When what occurs appears to match their expectations, they are likely to see this activity in a positive light. However, when students and teachers do not act in expected ways, this may lead the parent or student teacher to see the activity as confusing or even inappropriate and then to assess the activity in a negative way.

Whether positive or negative, both sets of observations often lead to judgments about the quality of instruction and its appropriateness; rather than to questions about what is happening and why. To understand what is happening and why, an observer needs a lens through which to look at the ongoing activity among members of a group (e.g., a class, a faculty meeting, a school, or even a bank) that will make visible the knowledge that members use to participate in socially appropriate ways, ways that enable them to gain access to knowledge or to particular situations in which they want to participate. This lens enables an observer to understand how members of a class (or other group) view and interpret activities, who can participate, when, where, in what ways, under what conditions, for what purposes or even with what outcomes.

Recently researchers (ethnographers) have shown that answers to such questions are necessary in order to enter an ongoing classroom (Where can I sit? What does it mean to "circle up?" When can I sharpen my pencils?), a new school (When can we use the bathrooms? Who can play in the small playground? Why do some students get to eat lunch with the principal?), or even to know how to make a turn in a new city (Can I turn right on a red light or left into a one way street? Is it legal to make a U-turn in the middle of the block?). Answers to such questions are needed if the newcomer to the group or place is to be viewed as acting in socially appropriate ways. Without such knowledge, the newcomer is likely to break rules that members use in conducting everyday life, and then be assessed as not knowing or not competent. Additionally, these rules are often invisible to members who just use them, even if they are official laws. The problem of entering an ongoing classroom was clearly articulated by a fifth grade student when asked to write about his classroom community:

> In our Tower community, we have our own language as well as the languages we bring from outside (like Spanish and English) which helped us make our own language. So, for example, someone that is not from our classroom community would not understand what insider, outsider, think twice, notetaking/notemaking, literature log and learning log mean. If Ms. Yeager says we are going to "make a sandwich," the people from another class or room would think that we were going to make a sandwich to eat. Of course we aren't, but that is part of our common language.

To be an insider, which means a person from the class, you also need to know our Bill of Rights and Responsibilities which was made by the members of the Tower community. And if Ms. Yeager said, "Leave your H.R.L. on your desk," people would not understand unless someone from the Tower community told him/her and even if we told him/her that H.R.L. stands for 'Home Reading Log,' they still would not understand what it is and what you write in it. If we told a new student, "It's time for SSL and ESL," he would not understand.

These words are all part of the common Tower community language and if someone new were to come in, we would have to explain how we got them and what they mean. We also would tell them that we got this language by reports, information, investigations, and what we do and learn in our Tower community.

In *Ethnographic Eyes: A Teacher's Guide to Classroom Observation*, Carolyn Frank provides ways that student teachers and others can develop lenses for seeing the patterns and practices of life within classrooms. Drawing on work in anthropology in education, she describes ways that developing "ethnographic eyes" help student teachers understand the importance of suspending judgment so that they can learn how to see learning in the actions of members, to acquire insider knowledge of teaching and learning processes in different classroom sites, and to act in professionally competent ways. By sharing her experiences as a supervisor of student teachers and the developing understandings of a group of beginning teachers across their student teaching experiences, she brings the reader into the processes involved in becoming a teacher in a new way. In each chapter, the reader is invited to engage in activities that will help them develop new insights into teaching and learning processes and to "see" as insiders in the classroom and the teaching profession. Readers who take up this opportunity will become more aware of what they are doing and what lenses they are using to "see" life in classrooms, and to develop a language of teaching and learning that makes visible the complex, yet ordinary, everyday work of teachers and students.

In introducing student teachers and their supervisors to ethnography, Carolyn Frank joins a growing group of educators and researchers who are exploring the value of using an ethnographic perspective in education. This group includes teachers as well as researchers who are seeking new ways of seeing and understanding life in classrooms. Two different bodies of this work will be particularly of interest to readers of this unique volume. The first is work that shows how teachers engage students in studies using "ethnographic eyes" in order to gain insights into the ways that history works, how life in their classroom influences what they learn, and how life in their communities can become sources of curriculum. Examples of such work can be found in *Students as Inquirers of Language and Culture in Their Own Communities*

(Egan-Robertson and Bloome 1998), in *Ways with Words* (Heath 1983), and in a recent issue of the journal *Primary Voices K–6* (National Council of Teachers of English) on "Classrooms as Cultures" (Dixon, Frank, and Green 1999). The second is work that shows how researchers and teachers can collaborate to make visible how opportunities for learning are created in classrooms with complex organizational patterns in which students become active inquirers and learners (see, for example, Whitmore and Crowell [1994], Taylor [1983], Taylor and Dorsey-Gaines [1988], Wells and Chang-Wells [1992]). This growing body of work, when joined with more traditional ethnographic research in classrooms and school sites forms, what Judith Green and David Bloome (1997) argue is a discipline within the field of education.

Carolyn Frank has written an inviting and readable introduction to ethnography that shows its value to beginning teachers as well as to their supervisors. In introducing an ethnographic approach for student teachers, she makes an important contribution to teacher education. Those who take the journey to understanding with Carolyn and her students will be rewarded for their efforts with new understandings, and new ways of seeing the complex and amazing work of teachers and students.

Works Cited

Dixon, C., C. Frank, and J. Green. 1999. "Classrooms as Cultures." *Primary Voices K–6.* 7(3):4–8.

Egan-Robertson, A., and D. Bloome, eds. 1998. *Students as Researchers of Culture and Language in Their Own Communities.* Gesskill, NJ: Hampton Press.

Green, J. L., and D. Bloome. 1997. "Ethnography and Ethnographers of and in Education: A Situated Perspective." In *Handbook for Research in the Communicative and Visual Arts,* edited by S. B. Heath, J. Flood, and D. Lapp, 181–202. New York: Macmillan.

Heath, S. B. 1983. *Ways with Words: Language, Life and Work in Communities and Classrooms.* Cambridge: Cambridge University Press.

Taylor, D. 1983. *Family Literacy: Young Children Learning to Read and Write.* Portsmouth, NH: Heinemann.

Taylor, D., and C. Dorsey-Gaines. 1988. *Growing Up Literate: Learning in Inner City-Families.* Portsmouth, NH: Heinemann.

Wells, G., and G. L. Chang-Wells. 1992. *Constructing Knowledge Together.* Portsmouth, NH: Heinemann.

Whitmore, K., and C. Crowell. 1994. *Inventing a Classroom: Life in a Bilingual, Whole Language Learning Community.* York, ME: Stenhouse.

Acknowledgments

I want to thank my friend and teacher, Judith Green, for first introducing me to educational ethnography. Carol Dixon and Judith Green read many versions of the chapters and helped to create language and ideas for the whole book. Louise Jennings and Irene Pattenaude created the phrase "ethnographic eyes" and allowed me to use it for the title. I am deeply indebted to the nine student teachers, profiled in this book, who have allowed me to share their written work, reflections, poems, photographs, and discussions. I also want to thank the principal, faculty, and staff of the elementary school where these student teachers were teaching.

My colleagues in the Santa Barbara Classroom Discourse Group contributed many discussions and ideas. In particular, I want to thank LeAnn Putney, Ana Floriani, Louise Jennings, Lesley Rex, Ana Inés Heras, Maria Franquiz, Marcia Rech, Rosemary Staley, Maria Lucia Castanheira, Marli Hodel, Silvia Neves, Teri Foster, and Teresa Crawford. My editor, Lois Bridges, has kept me on track and provided valuable feedback. My colleagues from the South Coast Writing Project, especially Lois Brandts, Beth Yeager, Eileen Craviotto, Cynthia Martin, Anita Cruse, Steve Flores, Sheridan Blau, Steven Marcus, and Jack Phraener, helped with many perspectives and ideas. I would like to thank The Anne Coffin Johnstone Memorial Fund, which supported in part the research presented in this book.

The faculty of the Teacher Education Program at the University of California, Santa Barbara, especially Sabrina Tuyay, Ann Lippincott, Marianne Caston, Jon Snyder, Jules Zimmer, Sue Hoag, Rosemary Staley, Ralph Cordova, and Ted Martin, made it possible for this research to take place as they contributed advice and direction. I also want to thank Betsy Brenner and Jenny Cook-Gumperz. In addition, I want to recognize the faculty in the Charter School of Education at California State University, Los Angeles, especially Cherie DeJong, Frederick Uy, Margaret Moustafa, Darlene Michener, Joy Morin, Carole Silva, Judith Washburn, and Allen Mori.

1

An Ethnographic Perspective

Aurora, one of the student teachers, wrote about the day she went on a neighborhood walk with her Latino students:

> As we're walking, one more student joins us. I am told that another student and her family have a Mexican candy store, so I suggest we go by there. We head for the candy store, and I'm in for the next lesson of this educational walk. The "candy store" is actually "M's" living room in a small apartment complex. There are incredible amounts of people there, children and adults, not to mention a couple of students from our class!! I am so stunned to realize that they are selling this candy, etc. from their living room. I am invited in and told that I can pick something for free! I just want to stand there and take this incredible experience in. This is like something I have never encountered and that's because I am now experiencing someone else's culture.

This book explores the use of ethnography with teachers and students. I examine how ethnography (the study of culture) can be a useful tool for teachers to use in classrooms by describing my own experiences with student teachers. I was the university supervisor for nine student teachers during the 1997–1998 school year at a university in Southern California. Because of my experience with classroom research, I believed that an ethnographic perspective was going to help these nine teachers observe classrooms more effectively, without making quick, critical evaluations or "leaps to judgment." These student teachers were adept at reading the patterns of classrooms as students because of their many years of schooling. It was my goal to help them hold off on reading classroom patterns from their personal perspectives until they could see classroom patterns from the perspective of all of the members of the classroom. If they could do that, they would be creating a base for informed action; they

1

would be able to take action, not based on their personal views of teaching and learning, but instead based on their observations of classrooms. That period of reserving judgment and interpretation was important for them if they were to make the jump from thinking like students to thinking like teachers.

Another reason I began using ethnography with student teachers was because they traditionally had difficulty entering the second of their two placements in this year of student teaching. Ethnography helped these teachers with that transition and enabled them to understand teaching and learning from multiple perspectives. Ethnography helped us ask critical questions about supervision, classroom observations, lesson plans, reflections, interviews, data collection, and case studies.

Ethnography, or written descriptions of culture, also opened our eyes to other meanings for "culture." As Lydia, a student teacher wrote: "Through ethnography I will be able to continue to learn about myself." Ethnography changed our thinking about ourselves and our culture. Michael Agar (1994) captures this relationship clearly when he writes how ethnography can change the way we understand ourselves and others. The term *culture* can be:

> something those people "have," but it's more than that. . . . It's also what *happens to you* when you encounter differences, become aware of something in yourself, and work to figure out why the differences appeared. Culture is an awareness, a consciousness, one that reveals the hidden self and opens paths to other ways of being. (20)

It is from this perspective that this book begins. In order to help teachers develop an awareness and a consciousness of a new way of thinking, this book examines how these nine student teachers changed in their thinking about classrooms through gaining an ethnographic perspective. The questions of this book are: 1) How does gaining an ethnographic perspective enable teachers to observe more effectively in classrooms? 2) How does an ethnographic perspective change the consciousness and thinking of teachers to expand their cultural perspective? 3) How does ethnography enable teachers to critically reflect on their own practice? I invite you along as I reflect on the journey I took with these nine student teachers as we created experiences and "other ways of being."

Classroom Life from an Ethnographic Perspective

From an ethnographic perspective, a classroom culture is always constructed in our classrooms whether we realize it or not. Students and teachers come together for six hours every weekday for nine months and create patterned and shared ways of interacting, understanding, and believing (Bloome 1985).

An ethnographic perspective provides a lens to understand these particular patterns of classroom life which often become invisible because they become so regular, patterned, and ordinary.

For example, when classrooms use "table leaders" to collect and pass out papers, a particular kind of belief system is created in the classroom (i.e., students are responsible for the classroom management system). It may have taken the teacher and students time at the beginning of the year to put this practice in place. However, over time, this practice becomes customary and routine, and members (insiders) are often consciously unaware of how the practices are woven into their everyday life. The practices of everyday life in classrooms become so routine that they become *implicit*. The challenge to classroom observers (supervisors, principals, student teachers, and teacher educators) is to understand and reveal these implicit patterns and routines. Ethnography can be used as a tool by classroom observers to make visible what members are doing and learning in classrooms and to record, analyze, and represent the particular kind of classroom culture that is being created.

As a supervisor, entering the classroom only for a few minutes and only occasionally, it was a challenge to identify the patterns and know what kind of classroom was being constructed. Because of my knowledge of ethnography, I understood this and used my ethnographic tools to look for those implicit patterns that created classroom life. In addition, I realized how beneficial an ethnographic perspective would be for the student teachers who were going to become members of these classrooms. Showing these student teachers how to observe classrooms from a members' perspective helped them enter classrooms as learners, learning from members the cultural patterns of different classrooms.

Spradley and McCurdy (1972) discuss what it means to enter a social situation with an ethnographic perspective:

> In addition to being more systematic, persistent, and thorough, the ethnographer consciously seeks to be more objective. He wants his account to be free from distortion and bias, to accurately represent what people know and believe. He realizes that it is possible to describe someone's cultural knowledge in a manner that can result in a caricature. Instead of saying, "These weird people believe in this strange superstition that ghosts can make them sick," the ethnographer would rather say something like, "These people believe in supernatural beings which they call 'ghosts' and which they believe can cause illness." To be objective means to state the characteristics of objects and events as they exist and not to interpret, evaluate, and prejudge them. (13)

For these student teachers to be ethnographers, observers of culture, they had to learn to interpret the actions and the talk of the members of a social group from an "emic" point of view (or insider's knowledge of the way things are) and hold off on observing and judging from their own biases. As an ethnographer, I understood that it was not possible for these student teachers to be completely objective. However, I wanted them to understand that the observer must come to grips with the possibility that reality can be seen from many different perspectives. There is not "the" view of reality but "a" view. Students will see classrooms one way, teachers another, and ethnographers a third way. In juxtaposing these views, we come to see what is real from a variety of perspectives. To understand that there is never a completely objective account is to realize multiple perspectives.

Multiple Perspectives

Learning about multiple perspectives is the starting point for beginning ethnographers. I have lived in the United States for my entire life, and I had a difficult time with the idea that there is no one right reality. Because I was not bilingual, because I never had to live my life differently in school than I did at home, I had trouble thinking that there might be a different reality than the one I saw and created every day of my life. I had reservations about experiences being seen differently by different people. Wasn't something either true or not true, factual or not factual? For me to understand multiple perspectives took help from a good friend who was able to talk to me about my reservations. It was not a quick process and took time. I had to be wrenched away from my mainstream way of looking and my "one-way-only" of understanding the world. It was difficult to see life from a different viewpoint. The world was always OK for me without having to know from a different perspective. What I did not see was that the world was not OK for some others.

Understanding students and teachers through ethnography began for me with multiple perspectives. It began with an understanding that reality is not a given but depends on the position from which you are standing (your angle of view). It is a more complicated way of looking at the world when we sometimes want quick, simple, clear, THE one right answer, and "plain English." It is a difficult leap. It takes time and support. I concentrate on ethnographic and multiple perspectives because as our schools are becoming more ethnically and linguistically diverse, there is more likelihood of cultural mismatches between teachers and students (such as white teachers not understanding the language and culture of African-American, Latino, or Asian students). In my experience as a teacher of future teachers, an ethnographic perspective helps students understand teaching and learning from multiple perspectives; an ethnographic perspective helps them gain an awareness of the power of diversity and how these differences can be a resource for community development.

Ethnographic Fieldnotes

To show that it is normal to leap to judgment, I talked to the student teachers about my own experiences with participant observation (Spradley 1980) as a teacher walking into a second grade classroom to begin my ethnographic fieldwork for my dissertation. I explained to the student teachers that while taking ethnographic fieldnotes during my research classes, I had learned how to divide my observations into descriptive and interpretive notes. However, I was not experienced in recording these observations in the field. My co-researcher and dissertation advisor, Dr. Carol Dixon, suggested that we begin together in a first grade classroom with Lois Brandts (Frank, Dixon, and Brandts 1998). In contrasting Carol's descriptive fieldnotes with mine, I showed the student teachers how my notes (see the following fieldnotes) only named events and activities in the classroom between 9:30–10:00 A.M. and recorded only a brief description:

> 9:30   Storytime in front of room
> 9:35   Discussion of reptiles
>   Lois reads *Titus Turtle.*
> 9:45   Lois reads as children predict.
>   Lois uses "active" voices as she reads.
>   Child advises: "He should have just brought the ingredients."
>   Ending: Lois asks if children know (moral, ending, main point).
>   Story: Friendship is most important thing.
> 9:50   Discussion of feet poster
>   "Think about all the places where your feet went."
>   Talk with others about where you walked this summer.
>   After recess we will write.
>   Now "Sit together and chat."
> 10:00 Recess

In contrast to my descriptive fieldnotes, Carol's descriptions were much more comprehensive, describing the action and talk of the members in as much detail as was possible for her to write. In this more complete description, the chain of actions and talk that occurred between 9:30–10:01 A.M. could be reconstructed:

9:30   "oh what a nice quiet group - when finished put under basket and come up front and sit on rug. ~

9:31   "What do you think we're going to study... frog visitors, frog toys"

9:32   All but 4 kids at front of rm - "How many have gone to creek? (Atascadero)

9:34   Timmy - "once I had a pet turtle...then he died~ Several more share similar stories

9:35   "I want to read you a fantasy story - about frog & turtle who are best friends <u>I'll Meet You Halfway</u> - will be on the 'Special Editions' table" "This year much older - more access to S.E. books"

9:37   "Nancy," "You're not here." "How can you be here?" Reading book to group -

9:45   S - "He should have just brought the ingredients for it" (cake)

9:47   "That's what being friends is - meeting each other halfway" "Talk in groups about what you did this summer-" "In about 10 minutes going to snack recess - doing something else 1st - feet poster" "What are feet for? - walk, balance" "Talk in groups about what you did this summer -" "Where your feet went - after recess -" "Write 1st journal entry about it - get in groups of 3 or 4 & talk" Kids scattered around rm - sitting on floor - mostly boy groups & girl groups - L. has kids who sat at desks, move to floor

9:55   L. comes over to talk briefly about 2 students

:57   "You need to talk about it not walk about it."

9:58   "Quietly go back to seats, focus on me "My reason for having you talk to others - great ideas, think about what you talked about"

9:59   L. introduced us, I said a few words about why we're here.

10:01   Dismisses by families for recess - keeps one student to finish pg. she didn't do

Just by comparing the amount of writing Carol did with what I did, it shows how much more data Carol collected. However, when I looked closely at the way she described the talk and actions and contrasted it with the way I did, I found that I also used "cultural" phrases that could have included my biases and interpretations. For example, at 9:45 I wrote, "Child *advises* . . ." which was a judgment on the way that one member of this social group was responding. On the other hand, Carol's descriptions only included the talk of the teacher and students and their actions.

In addition, because of her detailed description, she had information that she could use in subsequent interviews with the members of the class. For example, Carol wrote, "10:01 Dismisses by families for recess - keeps one student to finish pg. she didn't do," while I wrote, "10:00 Recess." By describing the dismissal in detail, Carol collected information about how this teacher's practice included consequences for unfinished work. Carol could then ask Lois questions about "families" and the ways she conducted recess dismissal. In my notes, it is assumed that recess is done the same by all teachers and students in all classrooms.

When I was teaching first grade, I knew that my classroom was not the same as other classes at the same grade level, even if I was in the same school and using the same materials. I never knew exactly how to discuss this or explain its significance until ethnography. Ethnography gave me a language I could use to express this principle, that classrooms are *particular* social settings, mini-cultures in themselves, that are *not* universal. Events are different in classrooms because teachers and students are different, establishing and creating their own rights and obligations, roles and relationships, and norms and expectations (Green and Dixon 1993). With ethnography as a method for looking at classrooms, I could now help new teachers understand the "situatedness" (Heap 1980) of teaching and learning; I could help teachers understand how even such a commonly occurring event as recess was not a universal concept and was treated differently every day in every classroom.

Learning to See

To help my students understand why Carol was able to write such comprehensive notes, I showed them the other side of our fieldnotes, the Interpretive side. I made many judgments and evaluations between 9:30 and 10:00; Carol made very few. This caused me to miss much of what was actually happening inside the classroom. A quick glance at my notes showed that instead of writing down the talk and actions of the members, I was busy jumping to judgment. This resulted in my not seeing what was happening during this event. Since I thought I already knew what the teacher and students were doing in this situation, and since I assumed I knew what was going to happen, I was blind to what actually happened in this *particular* situation. I was also thinking about what I would be doing later in the day. No wonder I had no time to write descriptive notes.

Already I can see how much time she is saving this year—this day—by not having to introduce her "way," her rules to the kids. They know her and know how to operate in her class. Saves so much time. She's right. It's as if there was no summer and the kids have started school without an interruption.

This is great. The kids don't even care about the camera or Carol and Carolyn. (Are they used to us or is it first day jitters?) This is the way to study "education," "teachers," "students," "classrooms."

Lois has the ability to get kids really involved in their projects. I forgot how difficult it was physically to tape inside the classroom. My back will surely be ready for my heating pad and a long bath tonight. The constant movement of the teacher makes it imperative that the camera roam.

Whether or not I look thru view finder:

Sometimes I see more not looking thru camera. Plus, when kids watch me, they don't see me, seeing them thru the camera. They just see an adult & a camera & it's no big deal, until I'm "filming" behind the lens.

One of my notes is a good example of how I was basing my interpretations on my own cultural assumptions as a teacher and not on data. I wrote: "Lois has the ability to get kids really involved in their projects." Many months later, as an ethnographer, I was able to write the same thing, but then I had evidence based on detailed description of the talk which backed up my assertions (Frank 1997). Ethnography was teaching me how to "speak from evidence."

In comparison, I showed the student teachers Carol's Interpretive fieldnotes on the other side of her notebook and how much she observed because her attention and focus was on describing what was happening from a nonjudgmental, unbiased perspective. Carol's Interpretive side looked like this:

kids are so serious about task!

music (radio - classical) playing softly in background

kids at table 4 having conversation about families

By dividing what was happening in the classroom from her personal interpretations, Carol was able to write notes that could later be used as evidence to back up any claims she might ultimately make. (Classical music was often played in this room during writing events; children's talk at different tables was an important way that Lois created a particular kind of community.) On the other hand, my descriptive fieldnotes were so crammed with judgments, interpretations, and personal reflections, that I was missing much of what was going on inside this classroom. My description was inadequate because we could not reconstruct the chain of events from them. I was just naming activities. On the other hand, Carol's descriptions could be used as the basis for a discussion with the members of the class since she was describing *how* the activities and events were constructed.

Student Teachers and Ethnographic Fieldnotes

In the teacher education program, we used an activity called "Notetaking/ Notemaking" (Dixon and Horn 1995; Robertson 1996; Yeager 1999) to help student teachers understand the differences between their own personal perspective and an insider, classroom perspective. Notetaking/notemaking was presented to the student teachers as an ethnographic tool to help them observe in classrooms. The student teachers were asked to keep an observation notebook and to divide their observations into two sections: Notetaking (or descriptive fieldnotes) on one side and notemaking (interpretations of what is being observed) on the other side. We then showed them either a photograph or a video of a classroom. In this way, it was hoped that the student teachers would begin to reflect on how their own personal biases interfered with an objective account or differed from the classroom members' perspective.

In order to understand more completely what it feels like to go through this process, I have included one of the pictures that we use with students (see Figure 1–1).

Figure 1–1. *Picture Used for Student Teacher Observation*

Take a look at the picture and write down everything you see happening. Then take a look at some of the comments that our student teachers made when they first saw the picture:

"The kid is happy working with the teacher."

"The teacher was working quietly with the child."

"The student is being tutored by a classroom aide."

"The teacher is having a conference with the student."

The first response is generally based on personal assumptions instead of seeing what is happening from the perspective of the members of the social group presented in this picture. Have you assumed that the child in the picture is a student and that the room is a classroom? Go back to the picture again and try to divide your notetaking (descriptions) from your notemaking (interpretations and cultural judgments and assumptions). It is difficult to observe without making judgments. However, if we understand that these judgments are based on our own cultural biases, then the difference between description and interpretation becomes clear. Your new observations might look something like this:

Notetaking	Notemaking
Male child standing at table	Is he perhaps six to eight years old?
Female adult sitting to right of male child	Probably the teacher?
Folder and glue on table	The desk makes me think it's a classroom.
Box in background labeled "Literature Logs"	What else could this be?

As you can see, there are questions that could not be answered. When using an ethnographic frame, the goal is always to generate more questions that require interviews or more observations to explore. Ethnographers would not make judgments based on one moment. Instead, if presented with only one photograph, they would describe the actors and the objects in use. They would describe how the members orient to each other and where they are positioned in time and space. (The picture in Figure 1–1 was taken by the teacher inside a classroom, after school, at the end of the 1997–1998 school year. The child was in second grade and was participating in a student-led conference with his mother. He was about to open his portfolio and show his mother what he had accomplished during the year.)

After presenting the still picture to student teachers, we often show them a video of a first grade classroom and ask them to do the same thing. We do not tell them anything about the video before the showing and ask them to write down everything they see or hear happening. A typical student teacher response to the video was, "It was chaos!" If the observers jump to judgment quickly and make interpretations based on their own cultural perspective, then we showed them how this jump was detrimental to understanding what was happening from an insider point of view.

Teaching Notetaking/Notemaking

1. Show a photograph or video of a social situation.
2. Ask observers to take notes and write down everything they see or hear happening.
3. Write their notes on the board or overhead and divide them into either "notetaking" (NT) or "notemaking" (NM) depending on whether descriptive or interpretive.
4. Discuss the difference between the two sides. What was descriptive and what was interpretive? How are you grounding your interpretations?
5. Have students practice NT/NM skills with another picture or video.

The student teachers became proficient at notetaking/notemaking. (The pseudonyms I use are Alice, Ana, Aurora, Helen, Josh, Lydia, Maria, Mary, and Sue.) One of them took extensive descriptive notes while she was observing in different classrooms and then later, went back over her notes to add the notemaking. Ethnographers call this "cooking up" the notes, realizing that there is often not time to reflect on the happenings in the moment. In that case, often our "headnotes" can help us with the interpretations. This waiting time was a good indication that this student teacher, Ana, was not quick to make judgments. Here is a sample of Ana's fieldnotes when she went to observe in a bilingual fourth grade classroom:

Notetaking

A child is working at the computer. There are fourteen students working at their desks. Six students are working with another teacher (aide) in the back of the room. It is an English reading/writing group she is working with—speaking only in English I see a mother working

Notemaking

The class seems to be really self-directed. The children are really on task and each has their own thing that they are working on. I am not used to seeing students split up into different groups for Spanish and English readers because in my class they are with one child only and she is helping the student with something in English. There is a baby in a carriage nearby the mother. I hear classical music playing very lightly. I can only hear the music every once in awhile when the classroom is really quiet. I stand up and move around the room to see what the children at their desks are working on. They are writing scary stories. The baby makes a funny noise with her lips and everyone in the class laughs and stares for a few seconds, even the teacher. I look at the group working with the teacher and on the board I see:

5) Yo *quiero* a mi perrito
6) Yo voy a *querer* mucho ami perro
7) Vamos a *moler* la tortilla

Spanish readers, but it is really good for me to see this because it happens in a lot of upper grade settings, and I will be working in an upper grade bilingual setting next placement. I really like the idea of putting on music during work times. I know that when I hear classical music it really helps me to relax and calm as well as focus. I think that it has this same effect on the students in this class. I'm noticing more and more that I really cherish the laughter in a classroom when it comes from a sincere topic or source. It is also nice to see the students *and* the *teacher* laughing. It's good for students to see their teacher. . . .

On Ana's descriptive or notetaking side (she used the left side), she only recorded the actions of the group and herself. By telling how many children are in the room, the sound of the classroom, the noise of a baby crying, and her own angle of vision, we have a picture of what was happening in this classroom. From this description it is possible to ask questions about the baby in the classroom and what it means to include family members. Ana described the language in use and who was using what language. She recorded what was written on the board, a fleeting occurrence in classrooms. She gave us this account all without interpretation, an unusual ability in a student so new to ethnography. Ana was also bilingual and was perhaps more aware than I was of how to look at the world from different perspectives. In her notes, she writes, "I can only hear the music every once in awhile when the classroom is really quiet." She did not write, "The classroom is noisy." Instead, she writes *from her perspective* about what she observes.

On Ana's interpretive or notemaking side, she begins her interpretations with phrases such as: "I am not used to seeing. . . ." "I really like. . . ." "I know. . . ." "I think. . . ." and especially, "I'm noticing. . . ." She had taken extensive descriptive notes (since she was not busy judging or evaluating as she observed), and was able to base her interpretations on the evidence she had gathered during the observation. She was "speaking from evidence" on her interpretive side. Ethnography had given her a way of collecting data and analyzing it afterward. She was learning skills of observation, inquiry, research, and reflection.

When working with these student teachers on their fieldnotes as they observed in classrooms, I tried to have them form their interpretations into questions. Later in the year, as Ana became more comfortable with the process, she began turning her interpretations into questions:

> He's distracted once again and he's playing around. Is he just bored or what? Why hasn't he listened to anything that the teacher has said? I'm not going to be surprised now when he doesn't know how to get started or doesn't know what to do when he gets to his seat.

And later, on the same observation date:

> I'm wondering now if he can really get the answer by himself. He seems to know what he is saying. I wonder if he just can't write it down or if he is always busy writing down everything that the person next to him has written down.

These questions and speculations came about because of her detailed micro-observations and notetaking descriptions of actions and talk among students in one classroom. These reflections illustrate that she was beginning to understand the distinction between describing talk and actions in classrooms and interpreting that talk from a particular perspective.

Summary

My intention when I started working with ethnography and student teachers was to help them see classrooms from the perspective of members (teachers and students). I wanted new teachers to understand how complicated the social interactions were and how different one classroom is from another. I thought ethnography could explain, as nothing else could, the complexity involved in classroom learning. When I first heard the ethnographic questions, "Who can do what, when, with whom, for what purposes, under what conditions, with what outcomes?" (Green and Bloome 1995; Mehan 1979) I thought this was the perfect framework for understanding the complexity of classrooms.

It was not my intention to talk about equity and social justice or even multicultural issues. I thought that American classrooms provided "equal" chances for all, and I did not question it. I did not realize that to say "American" classrooms might even include Central and South America. "America" to me was the United States and "the way things ought to be." I am only just beginning to understand how ethnography and those same questions of who can do or say what, when, where, under what circumstances, for what purposes can also support teachers in understanding issues of equity and social justice and help them explore "other ways of being."

(At the end of each chapter, I have added questions for further inquiry that will help you take your own journey as you see classrooms through an ethnographic perspective. After the questions are activities to explore how the ideas in this chapter informed you in your own situation. Finally, there are suggested readings.)

Further Inquiry into Ideas

1. From what different perspectives can we observe classrooms?
2. Why is jumping to judgment a problem for classroom observers?
3. Does observing through multiple perspectives mean that there is no "truth"? What is truth and how does "fact" and "data" enter into the discussion?

Activities to Explore the Ideas

1. Go into a classroom and take fieldnotes as if you were a principal. Then change your perspective and take fieldnotes as if you were a parent.
2. Go into a classroom at the same time each day for a week. What do you see?
3. Go into three different eighth grade math classes using the same textbook. Are the class sessions the same? How are they different?

Suggested Readings

Agar, M. 1994. *Language Shock: Understanding the Culture of Conversation*. New York: William Morrow.

> The key to communication, says linguistic anthropologist Michael Agar, is understanding the context and culture of conversation. In *Language Shock*, Agar reveals how deeply our language and cultural values intertwine to define who we are and how we relate to one another.

Dixon, C. N., C. R. Frank, and J. L. Green. 1999. "Classrooms as Cultures: Toward Understanding the Constructed Nature of Life in Classrooms." *Primary Voices K–6* 7(3):4–8.

> In this issue of *Primary Voices*, the members of the Santa Barbara Classroom Discourse Group discuss how they use ethnography in a range of different ways.

Spradley, J. P. 1980. *Participant Observation*. San Francisco: Holt, Rinehart and Winston.

> One of the two primary texts used by qualitative research doctoral students, this book details the doing of ethnography from a cultural and cognitive anthropological perspective.

2

The Neighborhood Map

Lydia, one of the nine student teachers, wrote about her students' neighborhood:

> All of the students in my classroom live in Island View. This neighborhood is primarily a Mexican populated community. Nearby, there is a local park where children play with parents sitting to the side watching them. Spanish is the language spoken. As kids play, adults seem to be socializing. It reminds me of the *placitas* in Mexico where people come out after a hard day's work and hang out and talk to each other. People's apartment doors are open, and Mexican music is heard. Clothes and towels hang from balconies. Parking is impossible. It's not very orderly. Bikes and other things are on the tiny lawns. The complexes seem really run-down.

Lydia wrote this as part of her "Neighborhood Map" which was an ethnographic assignment for the student teachers. The purpose of this assignment was to help student teachers construct understandings of their students' lives outside of the classroom. From an ethnographic perspective, this means observing people by looking at their lives outside of school and includes collecting information on families, neighborhoods, languages, experiences, and especially friends and peers. Sharing what happened to these nine student teachers during this activity, will show how we all broadened our definition of culture. Because of the visit of one student teacher, Aurora, we all "changed our consciousness" about ourselves and other groups of people and used our differences as a rich resource to experience "other ways of being."

The student teachers were asked to find the exact address of each of their classroom students, to find a map of the neighborhood, and to walk or drive to each of the houses in order to actually see where each student lived. Then, the student teachers summarized this walk or drive stating what it told them about

15

their students and the neighborhood where their students lived. Then they presented this summary to their small group during an informal discussion.

Micro-Macro Perspectives

The nine student teachers were beginning to see classrooms from "micro-macro" perspectives (Lutz 1981). By that I mean that they were learning how to observe the details of classroom life (by taking fieldnotes on the talk and action of the teacher and the students) and at the same time looking at the broader picture (by searching out information in the neighborhood). My own experience with micro-macro perspectives began when I took an ethnography class from Dr. Judith Green. She showed us a video entitled *The Power of Ten* (PBS). In this video, the camera lens at first focused on the hairs of an individual's arm and slowly pulled backwards so that more information was included in the shot, but with less detail. The camera lens widened and showed the people having a picnic on the blanket, and then pulled farther away and showed the city where they were living, and finally the whole earth could be seen. By making constant comparisons between the details of classrooms and the broader dimensions of students' lives, student teachers were able to compile more complete pictures of life for students in particular classrooms at particular schools.

When looking at students from this perspective, scores on tests, report cards, or observations from previous teachers are only the tip of the iceberg. Judith showed us a picture of an iceberg (Green 1992) and explained how information must be gathered from many different areas and perspectives. In Figure 2–1, the phenomenon of interest (either a student or a whole classroom) was symbolized by the iceberg. When looking from just one perspective or when accumulating surface information, only part of the classroom experiences can be seen. But when multiple sources of data collection are used, each collected from different theoretical perspectives (symbolized by the undersea vessels), then more of the phenomenon can be explored. From each perspective, more data is gathered and more information is available.

Collecting Data

The Latino residents living in apartment buildings in Island View were usually recent immigrants from Mexico, Central America, or South America and could live inexpensively in these buildings. The rents were low and many people could live in one building since the landlords allowed groups to live in one apartment. This was usually a temporary residence for families as it

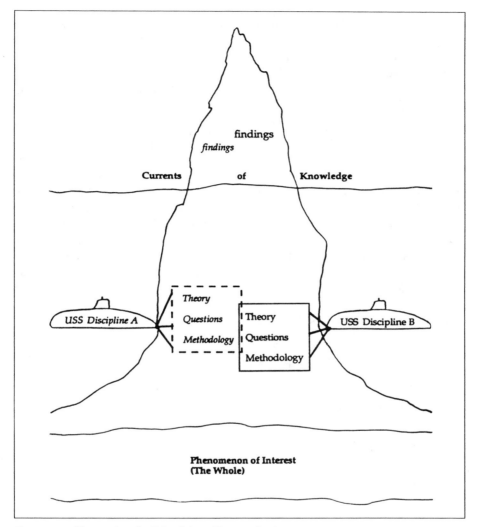

Figure 2–1. *Illustrating the Selectivity of Perspectives*

took about five or six years, after signing up for better housing in another area, to move away from Island View and perhaps another generation before single-family homes could be acquired.

In collecting information for their maps (a list of addresses of their students, a map of the neighborhood, possibly photographs of the houses, and a summary of their trip), the student teachers discovered the housing conditions of their Latino students. This neighborhood where the students lived was surrounded by a larger community made up of college students who attended the university. The elementary school where all nine of the student teachers were placed was populated by mostly minority students (78 percent). Seventy-four percent were identified as Limited English Proficient, and 89 percent were on free lunch. The community in which Island View Elementary School was located was 78 percent caucasian. This discrepancy between the composition of the school population and the community population was due to the fact that Island View was located within a college community made up of mostly caucasian students who attended the university.

Because the school was within walking distance to their homes and because the back of the school was a huge, grassy playground, the families of the students would often walk to school with their children and younger, preschool brothers and sisters. They would meet with other friends and sit and watch over the playground. Sometimes they would walk through the school and wave to their children in the classrooms. Doors were always open at Island View Elementary and the school gave the impression of being a huge Spanish-English-speaking family, even though other languages were also spoken by students.

Island View Elementary School (1997–1998 School Year)

Population   610 (K–6)

Languages   22 (LEP 74%)

Ethnicity   78% Minority

- 68% Hispanic
- 22% White
- 7% Asian
- 3% African American
- 0% (3) American Indian

Free Lunch   89%

Teachers   30 (12 Bilingual)

9 Preservice Teachers

The Island View neighborhood was in the center of a college housing community and close to the university where the student teachers attended the teacher education program. Most undergraduate students at this university were white and upper middle-class. Their "student" areas of living were separate from the "family" areas of living.

When Josh, one of the student teachers, did his neighborhood observation, the comparison between college students and young, poor Latino students was particularly interesting to him. This was an important step in learning how to look from an ethnographic perspective which enables observers to contrast one culture with another. Josh found the contrast between his Latino students and the college students to be influential in how his first graders looked at young adults. It seemed that this ethnographic assignment gave him the tools and the vehicle to be able to make this comparison. He wrote:

> What I kept thinking about as I toured these various neighborhoods was what a distorted view of college students these Island View children must have. As you drive through any street in Island View it is virtually guaranteed that you will see a lawn covered with beer bottles and cans. I think growing up here would give you the impression that most eighteen-, nineteen- and twenty-year-olds do little more than spend their parents' money and worship beer.

When I compared Josh's observations of the neighborhood with Lydia's description, I saw that Lydia focused on the smaller Latino neighborhood where most of her bilingual students resided. Within this small area, Lydia observed that it reminded her of the *placitas* of Mexico and that it seemed very different from the other areas in Island View in that "the complexes seem really run-down." On the other hand, Josh took the perspective of his students in seeing that the college students living across the street from his students "do little more than spend their parents' money and worship beer."

A Change of Consciousness

Aurora was a forty-one year old white, non-bilingual student teacher who lived in an affluent community north of the university. Aurora had reservations about joining the teacher education program at our university because of our special focus on bilingual education and because of her inability to speak Spanish. She also had reservations about being placed at Island View Elementary for her first assignment and in a sixth grade classroom where most of the students were Spanish speakers. Aurora's experience with her Neighborhood Map helped her to overcome these reservations and helped all of us in the small group to see the community from another perspective.

Aurora was working on this assignment one day, while observing in her sixth grade classroom, when four of her Latino students asked her what she was planning. When they found out, they volunteered to walk her around the neighborhood. They met at the local Burger King, and Aurora walked with them to their different homes. She described in both her written document and in transcripts taken from the weekly meetings with the other student teachers how she was invited into the homes of these students where there were many people and belongings packed into single apartments. She talked about how curious she was, and yet she did not want to act disrespectful.

> My senses are overwhelmed. I smell great aromas coming from the stove top, see too many people in a small area, and feel conspicuously like I'll be perceived as "checking them out." There's a part of me that wants to look around at everything I can, but the other part of me is telling me that would be disrespectful.

Although going into the homes was not part of the neighborhood map assignment, Aurora took advantage of this opportunity in order to understand the lives of her students in more depth. Aurora reflected on this experience and began to see the life experiences of her students from a perspective that was different from her own:

> I thought I could learn about their culture by just having them in my classroom, but I now realize that when they're in the classroom, they're experiencing my culture, not theirs.

Aurora was beginning to observe from a different perspective. In addition, she was reflecting on the changes to her own consciousness because of the experience of stepping into another culture. These changes happened to all of us in the small group and were some of the benefits of observing as ethnographers and discovering "other ways of being."

As the student teachers shared their neighborhood maps in the small group, Aurora told the others how one of her students invited her to her parents' "candy store." When they arrived, Aurora realized the candy store was inside the student's house. At first we were amazed, until two of our student teachers, Maria and Lydia, mentioned that this was common practice in Mexico and that stores were often found inside peoples' homes. Now we saw the candy store inside the home of Aurora's student, not as weird or unusual, but from a different viewpoint, one in which it was common practice and "normal" activity.

In our small group of student teachers two were of Mexican descent, one of Argentinian descent, four were of European descent, and two were Asian, one of Japanese descent and one born in Laos. Because of this diversity seeing events from different cultural perspectives was a common occurrence when the group got together. During October, we were learning about *El Día De Los Muertos* (Day of the Dead), a fall festival among Latino families where the cemeteries are decorated and relatives are remembered. Helen, a Japanese American student teacher told us that a similar ceremony is carried out in Japan called *Obon*. In Japan, this religious holiday occurs in the summer and is a time when relatives clean the headstones of their ancestors. By listening to each other's experiences, we were compiling a collection of differences, which provided a resource for newer and better understanding of ourselves and each other.

Different Angles of Vision

Maria, a bilingual student teacher who identified herself as a Chicana at the beginning of the school year wrote about the same neighborhood map experience from a different perspective:

> I remember growing up in my barrio and feeling comfortable with poverty around me—it was the norm. As I grew older I began to explore more affluent communities. These excursions left me traumatized—feeling less then. I was embarrassed of who I was, where I came from, and where I might end up.

In juxtaposing these student teacher voices, it can be seen how they constructed understandings of what they experienced in different ways. By linking their personal history of the observed reality of their students, they were reinvoking histories through these assignments and sharing it with the other preservice teachers in our weekly seminars. In order to engage in ethnographic events and observe from multiple perspectives, the student teachers had to challenge their own cultural assumptions, and through using an ethnographic perspective they gained new insights into their students' lives outside of the classroom.

At first, Aurora saw her cultural resources as having more value than those of her students:

> I see firsthand the love they have for their children and how they want them to have as much as my son does, but they have more stumbling blocks keeping them from acquiring the things I am able to acquire.

In contrast to Aurora and Maria, Lydia, a Latino, bilingual student teacher, demonstrated her awareness of the cultural resources of the community and shared this perspective with the group:

> It can be easily assumed that the neighborhood consists of people that are from a lower economic status. All of my students walk to school and they all live very close to each other which makes me think they must spend a lot of time together which makes Island View School a special school. This

must be comforting to my students to know they have friends or neighbors in their classrooms. More so than maybe other students in other schools. Going through the neighborhood, even though it is obvious that it is not a high economic status community, I got a sense of a strong community, or a community where many people know each other.

With Lydia's help, our group experienced a growing awareness of the family and community values that immigrant parents bring with them when they enter our school communities (Valdés 1996). These family and community values of cooperation and companionship were beginning to take on as much worth for us as the mainstream school values of academic achievement and school-based literacies.

Aurora continued to reflect on this diversity issue when, at the end of November, the students constructed another ethnographic event. Each student had to observe four different classrooms outside of their own rooms, one of which had to be in a Montessori school. The Montessori school, which was private and expensive, was highly praised by all the students as they commented on the space, materials, and quality of teaching. However, at the end of Aurora's description of the Montessori classroom, her writing shows how she recognized the special aspects of classrooms from multiple perspectives:

> One final comment though. I noticed right off that there was not a diverse population of students in this class. After my exposure to diverse student populations at Island View School, it concerns me to see a classroom with a student body so limited in its diversity. I'm afraid that some students are excluded from an environment like this because of life circumstances. It's a shame that all children can't be in a classroom where supplies and attention are abundant.

At this point in her written assignment, Aurora showed her understanding of the inequality of life in her sixth grade classroom compared to life in the Montessori classroom. However, as Aurora reflected on this experience there was a shift in her perspective as she awakened to the power of diversity and continued with:

> On the other hand, I also think that it's a shame that the students in this particular classroom aren't exposed to children who have different backgrounds that they could share with them. I see a lot of benefits to a diverse classroom.

As we observed in other classroom situations we were able to keep in mind that other classrooms were not as rich or as empowered because of their lack of diversity. The very fact that some classrooms *were* all of the same background left us with a sense that these classrooms did not enjoy the complexity of the cultural and linguistic abundance provided by diverse classrooms.

Over time, through the interaction of ethnography, the teacher education program, and Island View School, these preservice teachers helped each other see the positive dimensions of diversity.

Changes Through Ethnography

This ethnographic assignment of observing and mapping out the neighborhood not only increased understanding of students' lives and cultures, but

(Photos: Ted Martin)

Figure 2–2. *Neighborhood Photos*

also directly resulted in changes in student teachers' practice. Two of them, Ana and Mary, wrote about the consequences of their students having to live in small, crowded apartments. Mary wrote:

> I learned that often, because of difficulties in paying rent, many families live together in one and two bedroom apartments, which makes living conditions very difficult for the students who live there. I can only imagine how hard it must be for some students to finish all their homework or get a good night's sleep when there are multiple families living with them each day.

Mary was more aware of how her homework assignments were sometimes more difficult for particular students, understanding that some of her students' home lives were not conducive to academic, school-based projects. She became sensitive to this issue and developed assignments that were more open-ended so that all her students could succeed.

Ana's report on the assignment showed her how she could not always rely on "official" information from the office and that her students' lives were more transient than she realized:

> When I was looking at the list of addresses that I obtained from the office, I noticed that it showed that two of my students lived in the same exact complex, as well as the same exact apartment number. I asked the two children, who happened to be seated next to each other in the classroom, and George said that he lives there, and Christi said she used to live there. I explained to them that he was living in her old apartment and they looked at each other and smiled. I later told my teacher about this and she said that it was very common for these families to move around a lot. I then decided to ask everyone if they still lived at the same place that the address list listed and I found six children who had moved.

Not Just for New Teachers

Neighborhood Walks were not just for these inexperienced student teachers. Lois Brandts, the second grade teacher I observed during my doctoral research, knew that home visits were important for all teachers and students. Her email to me concerning one of her home visits points out the importance of getting to know the whole child.

> I am blown away by my visit to Mike's house. One of the old farms tucked back where you can't see it. Great spacious old place with gracious and wonderful old and new stuff to look at and do. They raise orchids in a HUGE greenhouse and Mike is an absolute expert. He has wonderful places to play

and hide and be an outdoors kid. He was so polite and thrilled that I was there, made me some guacamole from their own avocado trees, gave me avocados, an orchid, and a copy of a Monet that he and his big sister did. He is a bit lonely except when he has cousins/friends over. Does that explain his socializing nature at school? We are going to take the kids on a field trip to his place and you have to go and film. You won't believe it! Susan thinks that he might be headed for resource. Hell, I think Mike is going to be just fine . . . with or without the reading expertise. What a wonderful little human being he is. I suspected it all along, now I know it. I learned remarkable things and was kicking myself for not going earlier. But no. This is the way. First I held parent "brag " talks, now am going on the home visits, and then we will have student-led conferences at the end. (Email, Spring 1997)

Summary

The nine student teachers, while doing their neighborhood maps, used the tools of ethnography to collect data and analyze it from particular theoretical perspectives. They began to see life, not from their own perspectives as teachers in classrooms, but from their students' views of social and cultural situations outside of the classroom. They all gained an awareness and an understanding of how to observe their students from a broader perspective. The impact of the neighborhood map was crucial for these student teachers to understand how their students were looking at school and classrooms. Instead of thinking of their classrooms as the only academic environments for their students, they now had wider visions of student lives and background information to add to their assessments. At the same time, we all began to see the differences between the academic expectations that can be supported in home environments and the expectations that put constraints and roadblocks up for students.

In the next chapter, I discuss how the student teachers used the tools of ethnography to interview their cooperating (or mentor) teachers. The relationship that these beginning teachers had with their master teacher was an important step in joining the culture of teachers. I thought that an ethnographic interview would be a good way for the student teachers to understand how the teachers were thinking about students, classrooms, teaching, and learning.

Further Inquiry into Ideas

1. How different is the place where you grew up from the place where your students are growing up? Is it difficult for you to imagine what kinds of home situations they might be experiencing?

2. Why is it important to explore the students' neighborhood? Once you do discover where and how your students live, how does that information help you instruct your students in your classroom?

3. What kind of neighborhood support do your students have for some of the activities that are demanded of them in your classroom? Are there computers in the homes? Do the students have access to libraries and museums? Are the parents home when the students get home from school?

Activities to Explore the Ideas

1. Choose one particular place in the neighborhood that students visit (grocery store, video store, church, movie theater, playground) and conduct an observation using the practices of ethnographic fieldnotes (notetaking/notemaking).

2. Find out the kinds of after-school activities that are provided for students in your community. Is there a place for them to get help with homework? Are there sports activities, music lessons, or clubs for them to join? How does their environment (rural or urban) influence the kinds of background experiences they bring to the classroom?

3. Ask your students to tell you about their community. Do they understand social and economic factors associated with where people live? Do they think their community is a good place to live or not?

Suggested Readings

Heath, S. B. 1983. *Ways with Words: Language, Life, and Work in Communities and Classrooms.* Cambridge: Cambridge University Press.
Shirley Brice Heath describes her long-term ethnographic study of cultural differences in language and literacy learning in different communities.

Green, J. L. 1992. "Multiple Perspectives: Issues and Directions." In *Multidisciplinary Perspectives on Literacy Research,* edited by R. Beach, J. L. Green, M. L. Kamil, and T. Shanahan, 19–33. Urbana, IL: NCTE.
Judith Green discusses how many perspectives use similar concepts, terms, and techniques (e.g., field methods) but have differing assumptions about the world and how it works.

Valdés, G. 1996. *Con Respeto: Bridging the Distances Between Culturally Diverse Families and Schools: An Ethnographic Portrait.* New York: Teachers College Press.
This ethnography explores the lives of ten women from Mexico and shows how some immigrant values of family and community are needed in our society today.

3

Ethnographic Interviews for Teachers

Sue, one of the student teachers, wrote this reflection after observing a classroom teacher:

> It is weird how learning to "teacher talk" is for me like learning a new language. Here are some things that I caught (the teacher) saying that I should put under my list of teacher things to say:

1. When I count to 20, I want you all at the rug.
2. I still hear talking. I am going to keep on waiting, and your recess time will be taken away.
3. Billy, you are going to lose five minutes of your free time. This is not negotiable.
4. I really, really like the way that Susie is listening.
5. OK, let's clean out our ears. I need your listening ears.

As I worked with these nine student teachers, I realized that they lived two very different lives as student teachers. On one hand, they were students studying theories of teaching and learning at the university. On the other hand, they were involved in the practical aspects of teaching during their fieldwork in elementary school classrooms. At the university, the student teachers took on the role of students, one in which they were familiar and comfortable since they had experienced it for much of their lives. They engaged in discussions, read educational textbooks, and completed class assignments that were graded to assess their learning. At first, some of them enjoyed this part of their life more than their new role as a teacher, and they depended on their expertise as students to feel successful as student teachers.

During their time in the field, as student teachers learning how to practice the craft of teaching, their role shifted from being a student, intent on learning theory, to being a student teacher, intent on putting that theory into practice. For some of the student teachers, those with little experience in elementary school classrooms, this was a difficult shift. As a teacher they were involved in new practices of making lesson plans, managing activities for children, developing curriculum, assessing student learning, and scheduling events. Their role as teachers did not yet give some of them the sense of satisfaction or confidence that their role as students had given them.

The student teachers were being helped in this transition by their mentors, or cooperating teachers. The ability of the cooperating teacher to help the student teacher learn about teaching and learning depended on the relationship, or rapport, that was built between the two. I believed that these student teachers needed some way of understanding the thinking of their cooperating teacher in order to learn how to make decisions like a teacher. I thought that an ethnographic interview would be a good way for these student teachers to learn about the culture of teaching from the perspective of a practicing teacher. With ethnographic interviews to help understand this "member knowledge," these student teachers might better transition from thinking like students to thinking like teachers. If they began to know their cooperating teachers better, the rapport that was necessary between these two coworkers would be enhanced.

In addition, student teachers were beginning a career in which interviewing was a crucial practice. Teachers constantly interview students to assess where they are in their learning. Teachers also interview parents to get a better understanding of how to help students. Currently, with newer educational research showing that some teachers do not have enough information about students' lives outside of class (McCarthey 1997) teachers need a way of gathering more data about students through interviews (Barr et al. 1999). In an ethnographic interview, the ethnographer conducts the interview in order to learn something, not in order to explain something. I believed that this kind of interview would help new teachers gain more information from students and parents in order to be more effective in their teaching.

Ethnographer as Learner

When I first used ethnography to understand culture in my own research, I observed a restaurant in the town where I was attending the university. It was an established morning coffee shop near my home with many regular customers. I enjoyed sitting at the counter, drinking coffee, eating my oatmeal, and studying the people. However, I was not really understanding the culture of the restaurant and had to use an ethnographic interview to make sense of it all. I asked the owner if he would mind if I interviewed one of his waitresses. He chose a terrific informant for me to interview who caught on fast to the idea that I knew nothing and wanted her to be my guide and teacher. She explained the inner workings of the coffee shop, what she would name each customer (I was called "Oatmeal"), how the "tickets" or receipts were checked each night by the owner's mother, and a variety of other things that only insiders would know about this restaurant.

When I decided that the student teachers needed to interview their cooperating teachers, I realized that as students, they did not understand and communicate in the vernacular of the teacher. When they interviewed from their perspectives as students, they did not know what questions to ask. In addition, if a student teacher entered a classroom and began asking many questions, they felt that it reinforced their lack of expertise, their sense of not belonging in the classroom. They felt labeled as unintelligent and uninformed. In order to offset this problem, I told them that the role of the ethnographer is not that of a student, but rather that of an anthropologist trying to gather information about a different way of living. I thought this would be a perfect position for student teachers who were not familiar with the culture of teaching. Agar (1980) seemed to be talking to my students as I shared with them what he wrote about being an ethnographer:

> [The ethnographic interview is informal] because you are not taking on the formal role of interrogator. The ethnographer is very much in the one-down position discussed earlier. He doesn't know enough to ask the appropriate specific questions. In this early dance, the informant takes the lead. The ethnographer's role is to look interested and suggest a couple of turns toward the other side of the ballroom so that he can check the view from there. (90)

Thinking Like Teachers

Anthropologists use ethnographic interviews in part because it helps them to understand the ways of thinking of the people they interview. An example from my research helps to explain how this kind of interview helped my student teachers begin to "get in the heads" of their cooperating teachers. When I began my dissertation fieldwork, Carol Dixon and I went to interview the teacher in her classroom where I was going to be collecting data. During the entire interview, the teacher (Lois Brandts), talked mostly about the students. She went into detail about each of the seventeen children who were going to be moving with her from first grade to second grade. We listened to stories about Michael's difficult family life and Mary's older sister and brother who were in Lois' class in previous years. I was quite frustrated since I wanted to know more about the theory underlying her practice and what strategies she used to teach reading and writing. Carol Dixon, on the other hand, patiently listened to Lois talk. It took me a couple of years to understand that Lois *was* talking about her theories of teaching and learning: According to Lois, it should be all about kids. In meetings, when administrators would discuss policy, Lois would say, "The child doesn't march to the center very often." By listening to what Lois talked about (children) and by letting her direct the conversation, Carol was conducting an ethnographic interview. In this way, we learned how this particular teacher was thinking about teaching and learning.

Observing Like Teachers

There was another problem for the student teachers when it came to learning about their new role as a teacher. The student teachers would observe the classrooms, but they were not able to understand what they were seeing. As Spradley says, "Culture, the knowledge that people have learned as members of a group, cannot be observed directly" (1979, 7). The student teachers observed smoothly running classrooms, but they were not able to see how this came about. As they observed in the classroom, these nine student teachers realized quickly that they did not have the same expertise as their cooperating teachers. Maria, one of the student teachers wrote a poem about this:

> Maybe it was the stress.
> All the papers due on that day.
> The full moon shinning bright that night.
> Or all the cats singing in the alley light.
> Searching for excuses to calm my nerves.
> Searching in darkness without a clue.
> Impromptu has been my style, my savior in hard times.
> But on that hot midmorning, lesson impromptu wasn't my ally.
> I have to remember that I am still very young.
> I have much to learn.
> Georgia, you make it look so easy.
> You make it all turn.
> But with 10 years on your back,
> I cannot expect to be like that.

The student teachers tried to make up for this lack of expertise by copying the actions and talk of the teachers they watched. By doing that, they began to take on the activity of teaching, but without examining why they were doing what they were doing. They still were not understanding the teacher thinking that provided the basis for the teacher's practice. By doing ethnographic interviews, I believed that they would think of their cooperating teacher as an "informant" who could open up this new culture of teaching for them. By interviewing through ethnography, their classroom observations would make more sense to them. In addition, I was hoping that they would not be thinking of themselves as students but as learners or anthropologists who were opening up a new "dig."

Figure 3–1. *Josh and Mary in Class with Their Students*

Student Teachers and Ethnographic Interviews

I drew from three sources to teach the student teachers about ethnographic interviews. Then I adapted them to fit the student teacher's situation. The two text sources I used were Michael Agar's two books (*The Professional Stranger* and *Language Shock*) and James Spradley's two books (*The Ethnographic Interview* and *Participant Observation*). The third resource was my work with The Santa Barbara Classroom Discourse Group. This research group uses ethnography to research classrooms, believing that classrooms are cultures in which social interactional patterns are developed over time by students and teachers. This group uses an ethnographic approach and a sociolinguistic frame as a basis for observing classrooms as cultures in which each classroom is different. Even when the same textbooks are used in the same grade level in the same school, the classrooms are different because the teacher and students are different. They are constantly creating, moment by moment, different cultures, different interactional patterns, and different kinds of knowledges.

I discussed this theory of classrooms as cultures (Dixon, Frank, and Green 1999) with the student teachers. I explained how in each classroom, patterned ways of "perceiving, believing, evaluating, communicating, and acting" (Bloome 1985) were different. In order to understand how to perceive those patterned ways, and then to understand classrooms from a teacher perspective, I wanted the student teachers to take on the ways of ethnographers studying a culture—in this case, a classroom culture.

I explained how Spradley (1979) suggests that an ethnographic interview might begin with a "Grand Tour Question." This is a way of getting the big picture. A classroom teacher might give the student teacher a grand tour of the room where they will both teach. I showed the student teachers a variety of questions they could use to begin this grand tour:

- About space: Could you describe your classroom to me?
- About time: Could you describe the main things that happen during the school year, beginning in September and going through May or June?
- About events: Can you tell me all the things that happen in a reading group?
- About people: Can you tell me the names of all the office staff and what each person is like?
- About activities: What are you responsible for during an assembly?
- About objects: Could you describe all the math manipulatives in the class?

In addition, Spradley (1979) breaks apart the Grand Tour Questions into four categories. I explained these categories to the student teachers and gave them examples of each kind. During this first year of using ethnographic interviews, I provided the sample questions. However, Carol Dixon suggested that the students generate their own questions. Some of the questions might include:

- Typical Grand Tour Question: Could you describe a typical day in your classroom?
- Specific Grand Tour Question: Could you describe what will happen on the first day of school from the moment the kids come to school until they leave?
- Guided Grand Tour Question: Could you show me around the room and tell me what kinds of decisions you made about each area before school began in the fall?
- Task-Related Grand Tour Questions: Could you explain the steps you go through when you plan lessons for a week?

I told the student teachers that when they interviewed their cooperating teachers during an ethnographic interview they could ask them a variety of questions since "teacher thinking" included multiple and complex concepts concerning students and classrooms. Spradley (1979) constructed a matrix that could guide the student teachers toward understanding the many concepts members of any culture might think about. I adapted it for student teachers (see Figure 3–2) to use in their interviews and observations.

I discussed how this chart contained many concepts a teacher might begin to make decisions about when teaching a group of children in a classroom. If a student teacher wanted to know how a teacher was thinking, asking questions from the chart might be a place to begin. For example, beginning at the left-hand corner and moving diagonally down, the chart provides many questions to ask a teacher during an ethnographic interview:

Can you describe in detail:

- all the places in the classroom?
- all the objects in the classroom?
- all the acts in the classroom?
- all the activities in the classroom?
- all the events in the classroom?
- all the time periods in the classroom?
- all the actors in the classroom?

	Space	Object	Act	Activity	Event	Time	Actor	Goal	Feeling
SPACE	Can you describe in detail all the places in the room?	What are all the ways space is organized by objects in the room?	What are all the ways space is organized by acts in the room?	What are all the ways space is organized by activities in the room?	What are all the ways space is organized by events in the room?	What spatial changes occur over time in the room?	What are all the ways space is used by actors in the room?	What are all the ways space is related to goals in the room?	What places are associated with feelings in the room?
OBJECT	Where are objects located in the room?	Can you describe in detail all the objects in the room?	What are all the ways objects are used in acts in the room?	What are all the ways objects are used in activities in the room?	What are all the ways that objects are used in events in the room?	How are objects used at different times in the room?	What are all the ways objects are used by actors in the room?	How are objects used in seeking goals in the room?	What are all the ways objects evoke feelings in the room?
ACT	Where do acts occur in the room?	How do acts incorporate the use of objects in the room?	Can you describe in detail all the acts in the room?	How are acts a part of activities in the room?	How are acts a part of events in the room?	How do acts vary over time in the room?	What are the ways acts are performed by actors in the room?	What are all the ways acts are related to goals in the room?	What are all the ways acts are linked to feelings in the room?
ACTIVITY	What are all the places activities occur in the room?	What are all the ways activities incorporate objects in the room?	What are all the ways activities incorporate acts in the room?	Can you describe in detail all the activities in the room?	What are all the ways activities are part of events in the room?	How do activities vary at different times in the room?	What are all the ways activities involve actors in the room?	What are all the ways activities involve goals in the room?	How do activities involve feelings in the room?
EVENT	What are all the places events occur in the room?	What are all the ways events incorporate objects in the room?	What are all the ways events incorporate acts in the room?	What are all the ways events incorporate activities in the room?	Can you describe in detail all the events in the room?	How do events occur over time in the room? Is there any sequencing?	How do events involve the various actors in the room?	How are events related to goals in the room?	How do events involve feelings in the room?
TIME	Where do time periods occur in the room?	What are all the ways time affects objects in the room?	How do acts fall into time periods in the room?	How do activities fall into time periods in the room?	How do events fall into time periods in the room?	Can you describe in detail all the time periods in the room?	When are all the times actors are "on stage" in the room?	How are goals related to time periods in the room?	When are feelings evoked in the room?
ACTOR	Where do actors place themselves in the room?	What are all the ways actors use objects in the room?	What are all the ways actors use acts in the room?	How are actors involved in activities?	How are actors involved in events in the room?	How do actors change over time or at different times in the room?	Can you describe in detail all the actors in the room?	Which actors are linked to which goals in the room?	What are the feelings experienced by actors in the room?
GOAL	Where are goals sought and achieved in the room?	What are all the ways goals involve use of objects in the room?	What are all the ways goals involve acts in the room?	What activities are goal seeking or linked to goals in the room?	What are all the ways events are linked to goals in the room?	Which goals are scheduled for which times in the room?	How do the various goals affect the various actors in the room?	Can you describe in detail all the goals in the room?	What are the ways goals evoke feelings in the room?
FEELING	Where do the various feeling states occur in the room?	What feelings lead to the use of what objects in the room?	What are all the ways feelings affect acts in the room?	What are all the ways feelings affect activities in the room?	What are all the ways feeling affect events in the room?	How are feelings related to various time periods in the room?	What are all the ways feelings involve actors in the room?	What are the ways feelings influence goals in the room?	Can you describe in detail all the feelings in the room?

Figure 3–2. *Teacher's Decision Making Chart*

- all the goals in the classroom?
- all the feelings in the classroom?

Moving horizontally across the first row of the chart gives us the following questions to ask the classroom teacher:

Can you describe in detail all the places in the classroom?

What spatial changes occur over time?

What are all the ways space is used by students in the classroom?

What are all the ways space is related to goals in the classroom?

What places are associated with feelings in the classroom?

What are all the ways space is organized by:

objects in the classroom?

acts in the classroom?

activities in the classroom?

events in the classroom?

After our discussion of ethnographic interviews, I asked the student teachers to group themselves into pairs and interview each other about their younger days in elementary school. I asked them to use some of the ethnographic techniques we just discussed. The student teachers practiced with each other, and I was hopeful that many would talk to their cooperating teachers using the same practices. This interview with their cooperating teacher was not a formal assignment, since I was only exploring the possibility of using ethnographic interviews with student teachers. But, they could share the information in our small group seminar if they did an ethnographic interview.

Ethnographic Interviews for Making Decisions

Aurora told me that she had done a formal ethnographic interview with her cooperating teacher. When I discussed the interview with Aurora, she used words such as *informant* and *grand tour*. Because of this, I realized she had taken on an ethnographic perspective in her discussions with her cooperating teacher and understood the concepts those terms signaled. Aurora wrote about how she conducted the interview:

I found myself using the "probe" method of interviewing. I would pick up on one thing my cooperating teacher was talking about (when answering one of my questions) and that would lead me to another question.

Through this interview, Aurora began to understand the thinking behind some of the decisions of her cooperating teacher. For example, Aurora asked the following questions:

Where did you do your student teaching?

What do you like about teaching sixth grade?

What don't you care for teaching sixth grade?

How would you explain the overall atmosphere of Island View School?

What are the main considerations you thought of when setting up the room this way?

The answer to this last question brought out a wealth of information that student teachers might not have considered. The cooperating teacher talked about the physical constraints of electrical sockets for computers and the placement of the screen for the overhead projector determining where the "front" of the room was going to be. Aurora continued explaining how the teacher answered this question:

She has the desks set up in groups (mostly groups of 5) because she likes the students to work in cooperative groups. She placed her desk in the far corner because she seldom uses it. (I've only seen her sit at it a couple of times, and that has always been after school.) Even during reading or writing time, she chooses to sit at an empty student desk so as not to be away from the students. The desk works well in this area because there is a supply closet next to it. She has a couch set up right when you walk in the room (the back of the couch is near the entrance), and she has set it up around bookcases to serve as a class library and reading center.

Based on this interview, Aurora asked her cooperating teacher more questions about cooperative learning and grouping her students. She learned how this teacher was thinking about arranging the furniture in the classroom (mostly groups of five) according to her beliefs of how students learn best (using cooperative learning approximately 60 percent of the time). She also learned how important reading was to this teacher (placing a couch near the bookcases).

As the interview continued, Aurora was curious about why the walls were bare. Aurora told us that if it had been her classroom, the walls would have been covered with all sorts of "stuff." She discovered in the interview why this teacher left the walls bare:

On my first visit, the teacher had all of the bulletin boards (six in all) covered with colored paper and colorful boarders, but nothing else on them. My first impression was that the room lacked a "theme" and needed more "stuff" on the walls and bulletin boards. I quickly came to understand there was a theme and that theme was "Student Work". The walls of this classroom are evolving daily and are being adorned with the work the students have done since the first day of school. This class is definitely a "student-centered" classroom. This teacher did not feel it necessary to cover the walls and bulletin boards with her creations. She preferred to adorn them with the work of her students. This is not an assumption, because I asked her about it. When the boards were still empty, I asked her what she planned on putting on them, and she already knew exactly what would be going on each one, once the students completed those particular assignments. I was amazed at the thought and planning that went into each bulletin board. This was a great lesson for me because prior to witnessing this, I would have felt that every space should be filled on the first day of school with stuff!

Aurora also asked her cooperating teacher what she thought of team teaching, who the key people were that Aurora should know in the school, what kinds of decisions she had to make about the curriculum prior to the start of school, what main events would be happening in sixth grade, what happens in a reading group, and what she considers when forming a group. With all this information, Aurora was able to understand the classroom from the teacher's perspective and to see how this teacher was thinking about the students and making decisions about the classroom. Although Aurora might ultimately make different choices when she has her own classroom, she will at least understand many of the kinds of decisions that teachers need to make.

Ethnographic Interviews for Students

I suggested to the student teachers that they use ethnographic interviewing with their elementary students to gain insider, student perspectives on the classroom culture. I gave them an example from my own research. When I began my dissertation study, I went into a first grade class and talked with a young child named Carla. I wanted to interview her about her favorite storybooks, similar to the study done by Elizabeth Sulzby (1985) in which Sulzby developed a protocol for interviewing young students about beginning literacy. I wanted to understand the ways of thinking of a first grader. My objective in the interview was to learn how a child might think about some event in first grade. The topic of the information I gathered really did not matter. I had to suspend my adult view of looking at the world and instead try to discover the child's world from the child's point of view.

During this ethnographic interview, Carla and I ended up discussing, not favorite storybooks, but instead, the lunchroom. During the interview, I discovered how first graders go to lunch and I did glimpse the lunchroom through her eyes. When we were discussing what the children talk about at lunch, I repeated something she had previously said, "So, did you talk to your friend about meeting?" and the child responded with, "Yeah, like, see, pretend that we're sitting next to each other and she just got waved good-bye. Before she would leave, I would say, 'Meet me at The Big Toy,' or 'Meet me at the grass,' or something like that." By suspending my need to control the interview, I handed over the topic of discussion to the informant and in doing so learned how she was thinking about her world from her point of view. I also had new topics to ask about and was beginning to learn the language of first grade. I could now ask her what she meant by "got waved good-bye" (the lunchroom aide would excuse them if they raised their hands) and "The Big Toy" (a large piece of playground equipment).

Summary

As student teachers interviewed their cooperating teachers or used ethnographic interviews with students to explore the culture of their classrooms, they experienced a new appreciation for the way that ethnography was useful to teachers and students. In the next chapter, I discuss the ways that the cooperating teachers joined us in using ethnography to expose the implicit patterns and routines of different classrooms so that all members had access to the classroom culture.

Further Inquiry into Ideas

1. Who are the people in your school that you might consider "informants"? What information might they be able to give you about your students, your school, your neighborhood, or your curriculum?

2. How is the language of ethnography different from other forms of language? When you engage in an ethnographic interview, does the language you use put you in a position of inquirer and investigator? Do you feel that your questions position you as someone who does not understand or as someone who wants to learn more?

3. How might you change the way you interview students or parents with the use of ethnographic interviews?

Activities to Explore the Ideas

1. Tape record an ethnographic interview with an informant and then transcribe the interview to locate all the key folk terms your informant

has used. Do these folk terms lead you to identify the cultural domains of your informant's life?

2. Interview a student. Do you find that it is difficult not to guide the interview in a specific direction? Are all the questions about what you want to know or can you ask open-ended questions that help you understand how the student views their everyday life? How might you conduct the interview so that you can enter the student's world?

3. Interview a parent using Spradley's matrix. What areas of their lives might inform you about their children?

Suggested Readings

Spradley, J. P. 1979. *The Ethnographic Interview*. New York: Harcourt Brace Jovanovich.
This companion book to *Participant Observation* (1980) is a systematic handbook for doing ethnography with a focus on interviews. James Spradley gives specific guidelines for interviewing informants.

Tammivaara, J., and D. S. Enright. 1986. "On Eliciting Information: Dialogues with Child Informants." *Anthropology & Education Quarterly* 17, 218–38.
This insightful article on interviews with schoolchildren is written from an ethnographic perspective and considers the difference between interviewing children and adults, giving helpful ideas of how to enter the child's world.

Agar, M. 1980. *The Professional Stranger: An Informal Introduction to Ethnography*. New York: Academic Press.
Describing many of his experiences along the way, Michael Agar shows readers how to do ethnographic research from the perspective of a linguistic anthropologist. He talks about "Getting Started," "Personality and Cultural Background," "Beginning Fieldwork," and "Theory in Ethnography."

4

Making It Explicit

Ana, one of the student teachers wrote this in her reflection journal after she switched into her second placement:

> It has been quite a challenge getting into the classroom culture this second time around. I am more like a guest/visitor to them than a co-teacher like I was in my other class. I think the main reason it has been difficult for me is that I wasn't there with them the first day of school so they have come to know me as someone who is coming into their classroom and not as someone who is part of the classroom. I wasn't there to create it, build it, and share the beginning stages of the school year which I feel are really the important and crucial moments with those children. I am also being looked at as someone who does not really know everything about the classroom. The children know much more about the classroom culture than I do.

In the teacher education program, our student teachers had a primary placement and an intermediate placement. This meant that the student teachers spent the fall months in one classroom and the spring months in another. It was often easier for student teachers to understand the culture of their first classroom placement because they had helped to form the interactional patterns and the classroom norms and routines. However, in the second placement, it was sometimes difficult for them to access the culture, to become one of the members, because they did not always know the history of what had happened in the classroom to create the patterns of everyday life (Putney 1997).

The student teachers were expected to take over the teaching in the new classroom as "experienced" student teachers, but they actually knew very little about the interactional patterns, the roles and relationships, or how the new classroom worked. They were especially uninformed about the implicit routines that make classrooms operate: where the supplies were kept, where students were supposed to put their assignments, when to sharpen pencils, how to line up for lunch, who the "leaders" were in the classroom, and other classroom norms and expectations that "everyone knows" about except a new member. This is information that is often implicit, implied, and hidden from view because it has become so routine and normal. The student teacher's ability to gain the respect of the new students was dependent on their not looking foolish and unknowing and quickly gaining access to this information. Ana's journal reflects this concern clearly when she writes:

> I really didn't have the opportunity to hear at the beginning of the year, for instance, the class rules and expectations or where all the supplies are kept in the room. And although I went in and observed before coming into this classroom, and I interviewed my teacher, and looked around the room, there are still things that are missing, important information left out, and unanswered questions. The only way I could have really been prepared for the first day of being in that class and knowing exactly how things are run, so that I don't end up looking as though I have no clue as to what is going on, is to have gone through the mechanical aspect of the class with them. Now what ends up happening is that I feel as though I have lost some respect and authority with them. They really do see me as just another person that comes in and out of the classroom like the many aides, preprofessionals, and specialists that come in and out the door every day.

Ethnography as a Way of Uncovering Implicit Patterns

As ethnographers study different aspects of classroom life, in different situations, across a range of grade levels, they describe and explain how and why each particular classroom is different from every other one. For example, a description of the way students move in one particular classroom culture can be explained, compared, and contrasted with movement in other classrooms in order to understand situated classroom practices.

Students engage in this comparison of classrooms all the time as they travel from a classroom community with one teacher to another. Some students become adept at understanding differences in classroom practices; they become adept at reading the interactional patterns of their different teachers in different situations. They quickly "read" the room and the teacher and figure out what is appropriate action and talk and what is not. Other students, because of factors like language or interactional pattern differences or because of late entry, are not able to read the situation as quickly.

In this chapter, I discuss how these student teachers had a chance to enter new classrooms as "outsiders," as they moved from their first placement in the fall to their second placement in the spring, and how, because of their ethnographic perspective, they learned how difficult it might be to become part of already established communities. In December, the nine student teachers were asked to describe the classroom patterns of their first placement in order to prepare for entering their new classrooms in February. The first step was creating a classroom map.

The Classroom Map

The underlying assumption of the classroom map assignment was that the learning environment in a classroom was a reflection of the teacher's philosophy of teaching and learning. The student teachers were supposed to draw a map of the physical layout of the classroom and then describe five different "dimensions" (Jones and Prescott 1984) of each classroom (softness/hardness, open/closed, simple/complex, intrusion/seclusion, and high mobility/low mobility). Student teachers were asked to look for indicators of these five different dimensions. For example, cozy furniture, sandboxes, and messy art materials were considered indicators of a soft environment. Indicators of an open environment were decided upon by whether or not the classroom was student-centered or teacher-centered. The simple/complex indicators included variety and complexity in the tasks and tools available to students. Intrusion/seclusion considered the kinds of groupings that were in the classroom and to what extent the students could be alone.

As the student teachers began to understand how ethnography can uncover implicit norms and patterns in different classrooms, they used it to contrast aspects of their two classroom placements. The classroom map was used by them to compare these two classrooms. For example, the following description of movement in the classroom (mobility dimension) was taken from Ana's summary of her classroom map in her first placement in a bilingual second grade where there were eighteen students:

> There is a lot of movement both inside and outside of this classroom. As far as outside is concerned, the teacher holds P.E. at least three times a week for forty-five to thirty minutes. Inside the classroom the children are always moving around. She has them gather to the front carpet space many times throughout the day. They move from their desks to the floor often. They also move around to get drinks of water and wash their hands before lunch. She is not strict at all about being out of their space. They can move to work in another location without a problem. She has taught them a song with action involved. She often has the children get the materials themselves, clean them, and put them back instead of her doing all the work.

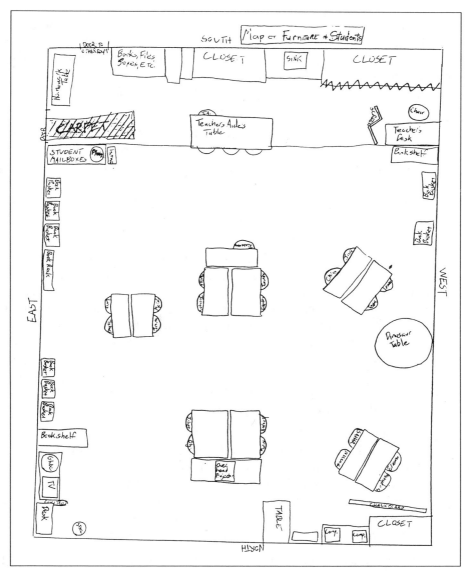

Figure 4–1. *Josh's Classroom Floor Plan*

Ana had a difficult time making the adjustment from her first placement in a bilingual second grade to her second placement in a bilingual fourth grade with twenty-eight students. In her classroom map description of this new room, which she mapped out after entering the new classroom in February, she explains part of the reason for a mismatch between the "way things were" in the first placement and the "way things are" in the new placement:

> This classroom is mostly a low mobility classroom. As soon as the children walk in from the line in the morning they are required to go to their desks and start working on *hazlo ahorra*. . . . Materials are usually passed out to them and rarely do the children get their own materials. The teacher is very uneasy about children getting out of their seats, and they have to ask permission to do so or they will get an "aviso" which means their name is written on the board.

When Ana stopped observing and began participating as a member of this new classroom culture, she was unaware of the significance of this seemingly unimportant detail of classroom life. She probably assumed that all classrooms operated approximately the same way when it came to student movement, or at least that it would not be such an important issue to her cooperating teacher. However, when Ana started teaching lessons in this new classroom, the movement patterns did not fit her norms and expectations. This small part of classroom life was important enough to the cooperating teacher to interrupt Ana's teaching. She stepped in and advised her on one of the "hidden" rules of this classroom: students need to stay seated and raise their hands.

> I actually asked the children to come up to me once so I could check their work when they had finished, but the teacher instantly stepped in and said that they need to raise their hands and stay seated. She would rather have the teacher be constantly moving around the room and circulating around than having the children do so. I really do not have a problem with the movement, but she feels that it is chaotic, and it is partly understandable considering the small amount of space in the classroom.

When students travel from one classroom to another, the same thing happens to them. If a child had been a student in a classroom where there was lots of movement and then suddenly moved to a classroom where movement was limited, the student's actions might be interpreted by the teacher and the other students as inappropriate or out of place. They might be judged as disruptive if they continued to operate by the rules of their previous classroom and if no one informed them that the rules for this part of life in their new classroom were different.

Ana, the student teacher, was used to one way of interacting with the students but had not been informed that certain aspects of life were very different in this new classroom. Her observations and interviews did not enable her to clearly see the difference in the movement patterns in the two classes. Ana told the other student teachers in our February meeting that:

> It's so much harder for me to figure out how things are done in fourth rather than second. [Second grade was] so ritualistic—like everything happened the same time and you could see transitions. But in this class, they really run on their own—I mean all the helpers—And I don't even know who the helpers are. I can interview the students or the teacher but I still miss something because *they just assume that I know it.* (emphasis added)

The differences in the mobility patterns of the two classes might never have been "seen" without the student teacher unintentionally changing the rules (telling the students to bring their papers to her after they had finished). Ethnographers call this a "frame clash" (Collins and Green 1992), a change in the patterns that makes the patterns visible. An ethnographer makes use of naturally occurring clashes in order to understand the classroom patterns of life in more depth. However, a new member of the classroom culture wants to be quickly considered a member of the community, one who does not create any breaks in the patterns. If we always assume that newcomers know the classroom interactional and instructional patterns, we may exclude them from knowing how our classrooms work.

The Implicitness of Classroom Life

Classroom life is built up over time by members using language to constantly construct interactional patterns, routines, and norms for appropriate actions and appropriate talk (Green and Dixon 1993). Some aspects of classroom life can be observed immediately on entry. As a supervisor of student teachers, when I enter a classroom, I look at the walls to see if there is student work displayed and to determine what students have done in past days. If it is an elementary classroom, I estimate the number of books available and read any charts that are displayed. I count the number of students and notice the arrangement of the desks. I quickly read the room in order to get a surface picture of what has been happening in that particular classroom.

Other aspects of classroom life become invisible to the casual, infrequent visitor. These implicit aspects are built up over time by the members of classrooms through their conversations. When Hugh Mehan (1979) studied a first grade classroom, he found that when a student wanted to talk in that classroom, the teacher did not make visible exactly how they should gain access and instead they had to figure it out by themselves. He writes:

> Students are provided with information about the appropriate ways to gain access to the floor *implicitly*. The teacher does not say, "When I name a student by name, or nod at him or her, that student and only that student can reply. When I say, "Raise your hand," or "Who knows . . . ." students are to indicate that they know the answer by raising their hands. When I say "What is this?" or trail off a sentence, or say, "Anyone," then everyone can answer directly. (161)

Implicit Knowledge as Ideational Order

The student teachers at Island View, guided by their new identity as ethnographers, and viewing from an ethnographic perspective, observed these obvious and less obvious classroom patterns in their first placements in preparation for comparing these patterns to their second placements. Before the nine student teachers entered new classrooms in the winter, we talked about norms and patterns that would have been formed in the fall and which might now be invisible to classroom observers because they had become so regular and routine. I told them it might be difficult to enter their new placement as outsiders. We discussed how *all* classrooms have obvious and less obvious patterns. Remember that Ana said she did not understand this aspect of the new class partly because *they assumed she already knew it*. Those classroom cultures that do not make that assumption and, instead, make the interactional patterns more visible will make it easier for all students to act appropriately as members of the classroom community.

In order to help them describe their classroom cultural patterns in more depth, I asked them to read a short ethnographic report taken from *The Cultural Experience: Ethnography in Complex Society* by Spradley and McCurdy (1972). In this example, "Helpers, Officers, and Lunchers: Ethnography of a Third-Grade Class" by Jean Doyle, the student teachers saw how to take one cultural scene, a third grade classroom, and write a cultural description about it.

This ethnography of a third grade classroom was constructed through an interview with a third grader. This informant talked about the meaning of three cultural domains, or areas of interest, in third grade: activities, identities, and space. With each domain, the ethnographer categorized the information into taxonomies. A taxonomy is a way of grouping the different areas of interest in order to make sense of them from the perspective of the members. For example, the third grade informant told the ethnographer in the interview about the different activities that took place during a typical day in her classroom, and the researcher then grouped them into the following taxonomy:

Activities or Actions

A. Working
1. Doing science
2. Doing social studies
3. Doing reading
4. Doing math
5. Doing music
6. Doing spelling
7. Correcting morning papers
8. Doing writing
9. Taking a speed test

B. Doing extra activities
1. Doing art
2. Making scrapbooks
3. Making pictures
4. Making things for the room
5. Writing poems
6. Writing stories

C. Playing games
1. Playing 7-Up
2. Playing Eraser-Pass-Back
3. Playing Eraser-on-the-Head
4. Playing Hangman
5. Playing Flying Dutchman
6. Playing kickball
7. Playing baseball
8. Playing Dog Catcher
9. Playing Changers

D. Having lunch
E. Having lavatory break
F. Having gym
G. Having show and tell
H. Choosing new officers
I. Reading *Reader's Digest*

After doing the taxonomy, the ethnographer prepared an analysis of the data and interpreted it from the perspective of a student in one particular third grade. What was discovered from this analysis was that in this particular classroom culture, student interests of the moment did not determine the activities. Instead, the clock was controlling how the time was spent. The ethnographer, Jean Doyle (1972), writes:

But what does all of this say about being a third grader [in this room]? It shows, for one thing, that their culture is structured and strictly regulated, in contrast to the freedom I had thought I might find. The day is completely divided into certain things to be done at certain times. The data revealed that what a child does in this class is not determined by interest or personal decision. Further, the class does not deliberate and decide on which activities they will undertake. Rather, the activities are regulated by the clock—they start and end at those points of time that students have learned are appropriate. (156)

I discussed this ethnography in a meeting with the student teachers prior to them entering their new classrooms in February. We began by having them describe the classroom cultural patterns in their present placements. As they described the patterns, I realized how much they knew about their classrooms and how looking from an ethnographic perspective had helped them understand in depth the everyday life of their own community cultures.

Most of them began by describing the temporal arrangements of instructional events (i.e., "First we begin with the calendar, then we have language arts. . . ."). Eventually they described the cultural patterns that are not easily seen by the casual visitor. These are what Spradley (1972) calls "ideational order" or the nonmaterial things in a classroom that are composed of ideas as they exist in people's minds. In one example, presented in the following transcript, Helen, the student teacher, and I discussed the underlying belief system of her classroom.

Carolyn: But the one thing that gets to the cultural belief system—the underlying themes—is that you said she (the cooperating teacher) is "Charney at work." But if I were not familiar with the book, could you tell me what are some things that show that?

Helen: Golden Rule, The Three R's, Modeling. She does tons of not only what you're supposed to do but what you're not supposed to do. Praising. She's really great—I don't know if I'll ever get this down—at being really stern about things but always having a softer tone—Like "Sit down . . . honey." Like she can say it where it's like, I'm telling it to you because I really care about you. She will say, "Sweetheart, I really don't want you to do that."

By understanding that classroom life is built up overtime by the *conversations* that take place between teacher and students and between students and students (Green 1983; Lin 1993), this student teacher tuned in to the language of the classroom. She observed and listened to the words her cooperating teacher spoke in order to see how she put into practice her philosophy of teaching. She described it in relationship to ideas in a book she had read (*Teaching Children to Care,* 1993).

Helen told the other student teachers that she was so used to this language that she took it with her to her new sixth grade placement. When she used that language in sixth grade, she got a different reaction.

> Well, I can't get out of that, and I will say, "Please sit down, dear."—and all these (sixth graders) say "DEAR?" and all of a sudden these kids are mimicking me!

Using Ethnography to Understand Practice

In February, after the student teachers had been in their new placements for a few weeks, we discussed their new classrooms and how easy or difficult it had been for them to enter the second classroom cultures. Traditionally, entering a new placement mid-year was a difficult time for student teachers. Surprisingly, most of the student teachers were describing good experiences in their new placements. I considered this an indication that the ethnographic perspective used by the student teachers and the cooperating teachers was making this transition easier.

As each one of them described their classrooms and how it compared with their old placements, I realized that they were now identifying themselves as "teachers" not as "student teachers." Alice said, "I'm feeling more comfortable in the role of teacher than I did in the fall." Aurora reminded us that in her first placement, one of the sixth grade boys had told her he did not have to listen to her because she was only a student. This time, Aurora said:

> It has been so easy. [My cooperating teacher] from the first introduced me as teacher not student. I really worked hard at not using that word "student."

There was another difference for the students in February. Although they were not completely comfortable with classroom management, it was not their central concern any more. They were now ready to look at other instructional issues. For instance, Helen was now concentrating on how her cooperating teacher questioned the students:

> It's no longer management issues. It's asking the right questions like, "What if you do this?" or "What if you do that?" or "Have you ever thought about this?" She's really good at probing them and really good at getting them thinking. And then when they ask questions she has these amazing answers. Like, "How do you even know that?"

The student teachers seemed to be using their knowledge of ethnography to understand classrooms from a member perspective. Sue told us that in the first placement, she did not know what she was supposed to know. Now, in the second placement, she had an awareness of what questions to ask and how to prepare. For example, in the first placement, she had difficulty with names so she prepared for that this time by practicing all day and writing down what they were wearing. In her first placement, she observed the teacher doing the opening but did not write detailed notes. When it came time for her to do the opening, she was confused about what to do. This time, she took detailed notes on how the cooperating teacher went through the calendar step by step.

Ethnography for Cooperating Teachers

All teachers' classrooms are not the same, and differences depend on those tiny, invisible, everyday occurrences that happen in the daily life of classrooms. An ethnographic perspective helps us see those differences and helps us to understand classrooms from multiple, overtime, and insider perspectives. If teachers, student teachers, cooperating teachers, and teacher educators know how to use the tools of ethnography to discover these implicit patterns, they can talk to all their students about how to live and work in their classrooms, how to gain access in particular classrooms, how to act and talk appropriately in order to be included in the classroom community.

The cooperating teachers became aware of how difficult it would be for their new student teachers to enter an ongoing community in February. They welcomed them in a variety of ways. Some had their students write books describing classroom patterns. Others had their students write letters telling the new student teacher about themselves and their interests. One cooperating teacher even prepared a bulletin board to welcome her newest member (see Figure 4–2).

The cooperating teachers realized that different teachers have unique rules about certain aspects of classroom life. Consider, for example, Helen's and Aurora's cooperating teacher. Her sixth grade students knew that pencils were an important part of everyday life in her classroom. She gave them new ones each month and liked having them sharp. The following description, written by one of her students in the book that was presented to Helen in February as she entered this new community, describes pencil rules in this room:

ABOUT THE PENCILS

When you need a pencil, there is a little box with pencils above Miss Jones' desk. If your pencil breaks, you can trade the one that broke with a new one in the little box. Sometimes you can trade if your point is a little bit low.

Figure 4–2. *Welcoming Bulletin Board*

You have to ask the teacher before you trade and get a new pencil. If you do not ask and the teacher sees you, she will remind you that you have to ask before you get a new pencil.

The example illustrates insider and outsider knowledge and its consequences for those entering this ongoing stream of life. This became visible because this cooperating teacher asked her students to write letters to Helen who was entering the class mid-year (February). After listing all the ordinary, often invisible dimensions of living in this classroom on the board (e.g.,"How We Do Attendance," "How to Get Table Points," "Switching Classes," "Our Computer Rotation," "How to Line Up For Lunch," and "How to Line Up For Library"), the sixth-graders were to choose one of those activities and describe it for the student teacher. The reason for this assignment was to help the newcomer (the new student teacher) understand community practices that guided their actions and interactions with each other. (Helen said that when she asked the students a question, they said, "Didn't you read the book?") The benefit of this assignment was that all members of the classroom had a chance to review these implicit rules and reflect on ways that learning and living took place in their own classroom, thus providing them with ways to access the curriculum.

Not Just for Beginners

This practice of using an ethnographic perspective to look at the implicit aspects of our classrooms is not just for beginning teachers. Experienced teachers also use ethnography to explore their learning environments. Lois Brandts, Eilene Craviotto, Sabrina Tuyay, and Beth Yeager, all experienced teachers and members of the Santa Barbara Classroom Discourse Group, are using ethnography in their classrooms every day (Brandts 1999; Craviotto, et al. 1999; Tuyay 1999; Yeager 1999).

For example, Sabrina Tuyay (1999) explains how when teaching a bilingual third grade class, she was being videotaped by her research group. The class was studying a unit on space. In one particular event, the students were writing planet stories. Sabrina went back over the videotape and made a transcript of what was said during this event in order to understand her classroom practices in more depth. She writes:

> Although my goal was to provide students with a chance to learn more about writing realistic fiction, it was not possible for me to predict or "see" these specific opportunities, as they were constructed in and through the moment-by-moment interactions of members of our class. It is important to recognize that only when one analyzes and further understands these interactions (by watching videotapes and transcribing the talk) do such opportunities become visible. (18)

Sabrina used ethnography to observe her own class as she watched and listened to the videotape of one of her lessons and transcribed the talk of the interactions. She described three Latino boys negotiating their language choices during a writing assignment. They first thought to write five things in English and five things in Spanish concerning their space story. As they decided how to do this, they spoke entirely in English. Sabrina pointed out to them that the third member of the group, a recent arrival from Mexico, could not join in the construction of the story because he did not know what they were doing. As Sabrina reflects on the transcript she made of the event, she writes:

> Here I was directing the boys' attention to the fact that because they had been speaking in English, Beto may not have been able to contribute ideas. ... What became evident as I constructed this transcript was my role in reshaping the small group's interactions so as to provide support for all members. (20)

Sabrina's actions not only provided support for all members, but by making the classroom practices explicit to the members, she was also providing ways that all members could see how to gain access to the academic curriculum (writing space stories). By making visible the invisible, by talking to the boys about how they had excluded Beto in the process because of their use of language, Sabrina brought out into the open a small occurrence in everyday classroom life that became part of the patterned ways of acting and interacting. These routines sometimes helped everyone to gain access to the curriculum and sometimes did not. By making them explicit, she exposed them for critical observation and evaluation by all members. As Ana, one of the student teachers, wrote:

> Ethnography has prepared me to think in a new way; a way that makes me think critically about everything that happens in my classroom.

When we become ethnographers of our own classroom cultures, by videotaping and watching the videos, by audiotaping and transcribing the talk, and by reflecting on reasons why we do certain things, we bring to light knowledge of the everyday life of classrooms in order to help our students gain access to the explicit as well as the implicit aspects of classroom life.

Further Inquiry into Ideas

1. Are there different rules for appropriate action for each event that takes place in your classroom or the classroom you are observing? Are these rules made explicit?

2. When new students enter your classroom, how do you invite them into the classroom? What support are they given to understand the implicit and explicit rules of the classroom?

3. Think about your classroom as having two different texts for students to read, an academic text including all the curriculum assignments and a social text including ways that the academic text is carried out socially between teacher and students. If you think about your classroom in this way, have you made available to all children the range of ways that they can read, access, and become part of both texts?

Activities to Explore the Ideas

1. Describe the events or activities that take place in a particular classroom. What are the different rules that apply to each event? How do students act appropriately during each event? Does the teacher constantly remind them of the ways of acting appropriately?

2. Describe what would be inappropriate action and talk during classroom events. What kind of talk does the teacher encourage during different events? How does appropriate action differ in this event from appropriate action in another event?

3. If there is another classroom nearby that is similar to yours, think of the ways that your classroom is different from that classroom. If possible, go and observe that classroom and see how students act and talk differently in that classroom as compared to how they act and talk in your classroom. Talk to the teacher about "appropriate" talk and action in that classroom as compared with "appropriate" talk and action in your classroom.

Suggested Readings

Spradley, J. P., and D. W. McCurdy. 1972. *The Cultural Experience: Ethnography in Complex Society.* Prospect Heights, IL: Waveland Press.
    Written for undergraduate anthropology students beginning to learn about ethnography, this book is valuable because it includes mini-ethnographies developed by the students of these two authors. The second half of the book contains such accounts as "A Little Gem: Ethnography of an Urban Jewelry Store," "Golden Age Apartments: Ethnography of Older People," "Thumbs Out: Ethnography of Hitchhiking," "Taking Cars: Ethnography of a Car Theft Ring," and "Fire Calls: Ethnography of Fire Fighters."

Philips, S. U. 1972. "Participant Structures and Communicative Competence: Warm Springs Children in Community and Classroom." In *Functions of Language in the Classroom,* edited by C. Cazden, V. John, and D. Hymes, 370–94. Prospect Heights, IL: Waveland Press.
    In this article describing Susan Philips' research on the Warm Springs Indian Reservation in central Oregon, the author defines the communicative contexts in which Indian and nonIndian behavior and participation differ, and describes the ways in which they differ.

Mehan, H. 1979. *Learning Lessons: Social Organization in the Classroom.* Cambridge, MA: Harvard University Press.
    One of my favorite books, which is inexplicably out of print, this is the story of ten months in the life of a first-grade classroom. The teacher, Professor Courtney Cazden, took a leave from Harvard in order to make the collaboration possible between herself and Hugh Mehan. In this book, the author discusses teacher-led lessons, a particular kind of speech event which eventually led to the description of IRE (initiation, reply, and evaluation).

5

Ethnographic Case Studies

Helen, one of the student teachers, wrote about the classroom student whom she observed for her case study assignment:

> I observed one day the one student who rarely fails to say after directed instruction, "Ms. Kakara, I don't understand!" Well, during every directed-teacher instruction, he was thumbing through his book, looking through his desk, staring into space, etc. It has been a wonder why he's so clueless! Ever since my observations, I tell him before instruction, he needs to focus.

Descriptive reviews (Carini 1986; Kanevsky 1993) have been used by classroom teachers to gather data on particular students who might be the focus of a child study meeting with others in the school. In this chapter, I discuss how the group of nine student teachers used this case study assignment to learn more about child-centered classrooms, how they used the notetaking/notemaking ethnographic practice of taking fieldnotes to collect data on particular children, and how they took instructional action based on their data collection and analysis.

The descriptive review assignment was used in our teacher education program to show student teachers how to collect data through observation for assessment purposes. The goal was to help them observe and describe how the experiences of children could be interpreted from the child's point of view. The basic assumption of this data collection assignment was that children are active meaning-makers trying to make sense of their experiences in school settings (Carini 1986). Building on the work of other teacher educators (Kanevsky 1993), our teacher education faculty wanted the student teachers to describe children as completely and as fully as possibly in many different settings. By understanding each child's interests and reasons for activity, the student teachers would hopefully gain insight into the child's way of looking at the world.

The written description of one child (a case study) was the goal, but it was also hoped that this collection of information would energize student teachers to take some kind of instructional action. In fact, many of the cooperating teachers who worked with the student teachers realized the usefulness of this assignment and suggested to the student teachers that they observe particular children. In Helen's example, she not only focused on the actions of the student and described what he was doing, but she took that information and used it to create a positive instructional action (by asking the student to focus just prior to a teacher-directed lesson). In another example, the school psychologist thought the information was so valuable that she asked the student teacher if the observation notes could be used at the child study meeting.

The case studies required the student teachers to use an ethnographic perspective of looking overtime (observing for many weeks or months), looking from an insider's perspective, and looking at multiple social situations. It was another way of showing them how to gather multiple sources of information before making instructional decisions or how not to jump to judgment too soon. In addition, they were encouraged to take on the role of researchers and to become notetakers/notemakers when gathering data for their account of one child.

This assignment allowed them to categorize multiple perspectives in the process of doing the assignment. For example, students were asked to break down their observations into particular characteristics, or facets of personality (see the following list). They had to describe the child physically, emotionally, socially, and academically. By understanding the whole child interacting with other whole children inside and outside the classroom, student teachers began to see their students from the child's point of view.

The Descriptive Review

1. Physical presence and gesture
2. Disposition
3. Relationships with children and adults
4. Activities and interests
5. Formal learning (Kanevsky 1993)

Speaking from Evidence

The multiple perspectives for this assignment were not limited to different aspects of the child's personality. In addition to observing the child in various academic and social contexts (during a language arts lesson, a math lesson, or at recess), student teachers were also able to view the students during different configurations of student gatherings (whole group, small group, individual). For example, Ana wrote thirty pages of fieldnotes (notetaking/notemaking) during the eight observations for her student. Ana completed two language arts observations, three math observations, one social studies observation, and two recess observations (see the following list). During those observations she documented whether or not the child was engaged in whole group activities, small group work, or working individually.

Ana's Observations of Sam

Observation Activity	Configuration of Group
1. Language arts	Whole group
2. Math lesson	Whole group then small group
3. Math lesson	Whole group at desks
4. Math lesson	Independent
5. Language arts	Whole group on rug
6. Social studies	Small group
7. Recess	Lines
8. Recess	Whole group

From this collection of information, gathered from her notetaking/notemaking fieldnotes as she observed in the classroom, Ana was able to "speak from evidence" and write in her descriptive review that Sam, her case study child, "works very well on his own and is an independent worker. He does not need much direction when he is working on drill type exercises." This claim was not a quick judgment but was arrived at after an exhaustive data collection process of doing participant observation and fieldnote taking, analyzing the notes, and comparing and contrasting time periods. She interpreted the evidence to mean that when Sam was working by himself he accomplished more work than when working with other children and concluded that he was "an independent worker."

When looking at Ana's fieldnotes, it can be seen how she came to this conclusion. During the second observation, she took descriptive notes about Sam and another student working together on a math game but having a dispute over the materials. Then she wrote on her notemaking side:

He's playing leepaway with the dice from his partner. He wants all the material and doesn't want to share them with (his partner). I've noticed that Sam may have a problem working with other students. We'll see what develops from this.

By explicitly making her hypothesis a guess rather than a fact, Ana focused her research so that she might collect information about that particular question (Does Sam have a problem working with other students?). This meant that she would look for information that would either agree or disagree with her guess and perhaps not look at other areas. In this way, she was able to answer one question in depth. Because she was willing to put off an immediate answer to this question, she was able to gather more information until a judgment could be made.

In another instance of the same event, Ana described how Sam talked to his partner: "Your turn. Hellooo!" Then she wrote on her notemaking side: "very duh [sarcastic] kind of tone he is using to his partner. Like hello wake up. A little rude if you ask me." By adding information on how Sam is working with other students, Ana is slowly collecting evidence for her inquiry.

During the third observation (see p. 57), an activity which involved the other students, Ana noted that "Sam covers his ears with both hands. He is turning his body around and head. He crawls on all fours on the floor. He is on his knees now." On the notemaking side she wrote: "He seems to be annoyed now and wants some kind of silence. He doesn't want to hear everyone talking. He's definitely not participating with the rest of the class."

On the fourth observation (see p. 57, which shows the students working independently), Ana observed that Sam "has worked on the worksheet doing the first four problems in three minutes. He has not said a word to anyone the whole time he has been sitting at his desk." On her notemaking side she wrote: "He's really on task. He usually is when he first starts working at the desk by himself. He's working really well, and he seems to know what he is doing." Because of all the evidence Ana collected through her notetaking/notemaking observations, she interpreted the information and described Sam as an independent worker.

This interpretation was valuable information and could possibly lead to instructional consequences. Now that she had made the judgment that he was an independent worker, she could help him develop social strategies to work with others in class on academic assignments. Realizing that he worked better by himself would be an indication that some children need independent time and do not always work best with their peers. The descriptive review in conjunction with the practice of notetaking/notemaking was helping the student teachers learn how to speak from evidence and how to take instructional action once judgments had been made. It was also helping them to see how different children learn in different ways.

Because the student teachers used the practice of notetaking/notemaking to observe one individual student, they were able to write down exactly what the actions and talk were on the notetaking side of their fieldnotes and then interpret them on the other side. Additionally, by engaging in this process, they could reflect on why they observed certain things or why they asked particular questions thereby beginning to use and understand inquiry and research processes. For example, because of her interest in the way Sam worked with others inside the classroom, Ana was also interested in Sam's play at recess. She writes on her notemaking side:

> I really wanted to find out more about this student at play. I have seen him play on the playground, but I knew there was more to it. I knew that there was a lot of fantasy play going on, so I thought it would be really neat to find out what they were doing by asking him and him telling me in his own words.

In this example, Ana explored the reasons why she was interested in the child's play and recognized that she could discover what was really happening at recess by asking the child and hearing him tell her in his own words. She understood that there is a difference between what adults interpret as they observe children at recess and what the children actually are intending to do at recess. She was recognizing the difference between an insider's view and an outsider's view.

In order to explore this in more depth, Ana engaged in an interview with Sam to discover the fantasy:

NOTETAKING

Ana: "What are you going to do at recess?"

Sam: "I'm going to go camping."

Ana: "You are going camping! Where?"

Sam: "In the forest."

Ana: "Where is that?"

Sam: "Way back in the field."

Ana: "Who is going camping with you?"

Sam: (lists a lot of students' names)

> [He gets a juice out of his backpack and closes his backpack up. He starts walking toward the door.]

Sam: "Yup we are going camping. It's time to go camping."

[He starts walking faster and faster and now he is running. He's swinging his arms in the air. He runs out the door. He is gone.]

On the notemaking side of Ana's fieldnotes, she interprets, evaluates, and questions what happened on her notetaking side. In this way and in order to discover the answers to all she wonders about, she opens the door to more ethnographic research and more focused interviews and observations. She writes:

NOTEMAKING

I thought the camping was really cute! I don't think I would have gotten that from watching them do this for weeks and weeks. I wonder if they use food items, like the juice, when they are "camping"? I wonder if they are using it during their play or if it's for his own pleasure? I do notice that he does take something out to recess with him almost every day.

Ana comments that just observing children does not always reveal all the information, and at some point the investigator has to sit down with the informant and ask them what things mean. She was discovering and using the valuable practice of collecting information from other people, not just from written texts. Spradley (1979) and Agar (1994) agree with this, and as I wrote in the previous chapter on interviews, Spradley says, "Culture, the knowledge that people have learned as members of a group, cannot be observed directly" (7). As I observed these nine student teachers and reflected on my own research, I realized that both interviewing and observing were important aspects of doing ethnography and that one was not complete without the other.

Choosing Students to Observe

The student teachers were asked to begin the descriptive review by choosing three different students to observe on the first day they entered their first classroom placement. As Aurora wrote, this was not an easy task:

This process began for me on September 4, 1997. Not only is this the day that I am assuming a new identity (that of student teacher), but I am starting this day with an assignment on my mind. The assignment is to choose three students from the class and then narrow these choices down to one that "interests" me. What a challenge! At this point, naturally, they all interest me. I am aware of twenty-six sets of eyes on me. They are looking a little puzzled. I am sure they are wondering who I am as I stand in the rear of the classroom looking and feeling a little bewildered. I take the opportunity to "break the ice" as the teacher lingers outside the door welcoming a new student to the school and talking to her mother. I introduce myself to the class and explain my position in the classroom. I still feel their stare. A few smile, but most look a bit bewildered.

The student teachers made decisions about which child to choose for their observations based on how the student caught their attention in some way. Josh picked Ben because "he naturally attracts the attention of everyone in the room." Mary chose Mike because "I noticed his eagerness for learning since the first day of school."

As these student teachers wrote up their accounts of each child, they sometimes realized how different their impressions were *after* the data collection than when they first chose the child. As Alice writes:

> Would I focus on EK from Iceland, TC from Cambodia, SH from Afghanistan, HK from Korea or NG from Germany? Eventually I decided to study AK. Why? Because he is simply so darn charming! His eyes are bright and alive, his eagerness and joy are contagious. In addition, I thought it would be particularly interesting since I am not very familiar with the Indian culture. After selecting AK for this study though, I began to feel a bit guilty about my choice, as there are so many other students in our class who are very needy and would perhaps benefit from the attention. Yet the image I have of AK has evolved over time due to these observations. I originally saw him as a very happy, healthy, energetic young boy. I now see that he is far more complicated.

Alice provides insight into why teachers sometimes think they understand their students while not really taking into account the complexities of their lives (McCarthey 1997). She continues to give evidence of her changed understandings brought about by taking the time to write down the actual words that were spoken by the student:

> For example, he has language weaknesses—the depth of which I did not see before. It was easy not to notice them since he comes across as being so bright. While listening to him try to express a thought or explain something, my mind would jump ahead, and fill in what he was trying (or what I thought he was trying) to say. I was reading his eyes, his gestures and his facial expressions, then guessing by taking the context into account. It was only when I wrote down his comments verbatim one morning that I realized how much he struggles with the English language. He is so eager and proud to share things with the class, even though it is difficult for him. I am also seeing that his emotional life is more complicated than I had originally thought. I see some sadnesses and weaknesses that were not apparent at first. Some I understand; others I am hoping to in the future.

Alice's reflections help to explain how teachers get caught up in the whirlwind of the everyday life in classrooms—when events speed by. Alice's reflections help to explain how we do not really understand what is happening until we stop the action by some means (videotape, audiotape, or fieldnotes) and actually analyze the events moment by moment. By doing this, Alice illustrates the connections that can develop between teacher and student when teachers look from the child's perspective and understand their complicated lives.

Another student teacher, Maria, had a similar experience in getting close to her student. She chose her case study student because of the similarities between the classroom student and the student teacher's background: "My initial attraction to Lily was her resemblance to my niece. Her dark skin color, regional accent, and economic status were familiar to my own personal background." Maria explains how this influenced her observation of Lily and explored how this connection with one child can enhance educational practice:

> As a result of Lucy's phenotypic resemblance I immediately felt a sense of protectiveness for her. I look at her mother and see my sister-in-law. I see her clothes and am reminded of myself as a child. I recognize that this fact colors my perspective. I cannot stop myself from caring, from seeking ways to help her. As a student teacher and researcher, my first intention is to explore the best methods to support Lucy's growth in education. I hope this descriptive review will aid this effort.

Physical Presence and Gesture

The student teachers focused on different aspects of their case study child when describing physical presence. Alice concentrated on watching how her student sat during rug time:

> During rug time, for example, there are many styles of sitting. Some students slouch, others have a tendency to sprawl or even lie down if given the opportunity. Some students can't hold still, others are constantly fussing with something (their sweater, their neighbor's hair, etc.). In contrast is AK. He always sits in the front row, directly in front of the teacher if possible. While other students wander and drift before finally settling down, AK goes directly to his favorite spot. He sits straight and tall, legs crossed, hands in lap, eyes fixed on the teacher. Fingers are held together, and movements are very precise. There is no extraneous movement. Gestures are purposeful.

In her description of how AK sits on the rug, Alice shows how this assignment has given her the chance to observe the micro (as opposed to macro) aspects of classroom life and focus on one facet of one child for one specific event. While doing this, the student teachers found that they saw the classroom world from the child's perspective. In addition, they were seeing the differences between one social situation in the classroom (calendar time) and another (writing workshop) and how the ways for students to act appropriately changed from one event to another (Green and Wallat 1981).

Remember Ana's student who was an independent worker? Ana also found herself caring for him and "seeking ways to help." Ana was observing Sam during math. He knew the answer to a question the teacher asked and was trying to get the teacher's attention. Ana described what happened in her fieldnotes:

NOTETAKING

He points at the number line with his right hand index finger. Moves his finger to the right in the air. He turns his head and is looking at the student giving the equation. He raises his hand and starts moving it back and forth quickly. His fingers are moving, and his body is swaying back and forth as well. Sam: "Uugh, uugh. I have one. I have one."

Ana notices that Sam is trying to get the teacher's attention so that he can share his answer. Then she interprets this event on her notemaking side:

He is really excited now. He is moving his hand frantically. I hope the teacher calls on him soon before he has a ♥ attack.

Ana was experiencing the same thing that Maria had written about when concentrating on just one child. Maria had chosen her case study child because of the similarities in backgrounds but discovered that when focusing on just one child, "I cannot stop myself from caring." Similarly, as Ana observed Sam sitting on the rug trying to gain the teacher's attention, she found herself hoping that the teacher would call on Sam. She writes:

NOTETAKING

Sam drops his hand that was raised to the ground. "Oohhh." He closes his eyes for a few seconds and closes his mouth tightly. He drops his body off of his two feet he was sitting on. He places his bottom on the floor now where before it was elevated from the floor.

NOTEMAKING

Oh No! She never called on him. Oh well, there were so many kids that wanted to be called on. I'm just focusing on him, so I feel badly for him. He looks really sad and depressed because he was never called on. He seems to be pouting and giving some dirty looks to the teacher. His whole body has just shown what he is feeling, like it wasn't really fair that he never got called on to say his equation with the number 13.

Summary

These student teachers became more knowledgeable about classrooms and students as they took ethnographic fieldnotes for their descriptive reviews. They learned how to observe (through notetaking/notemaking fieldnotes), what to observe (different contexts and social situations), and from what perspectives (the child's, the student teachers, the adults, etc.). In addition to using these ethnographic and sociolinguistic research practices, the student teachers came to understand that the interpretation of the observation is in part dependent on the perspective of the observer, the angle of vision. For example, Maria told me that as she was sitting in class observing and drawing her maps, her perspective was changing. When she first started observing, she was looking from the perspective of an ethnographer or participant observer. However, she said that once she had taught a lesson, once she had been the teacher in charge and up in front of the group leading the calendar activity, then her observations changed. Afterwards, her fieldnotes included a new awareness of the perspective of the teacher. She said the ability to observe in her classroom was dependent on the observer being up in front, in that position, and knowing what it felt like to be the classroom teacher.

Further Inquiry into Ideas

1. Why is it important to support our interpretations with evidence?
2. How many different perspectives can we use when we observe students?
3. How can we involve the student in the observation?
4. Often by focusing on one child, we gain insights into how all children learn. Through your experiences with the following activities, what have you learned about learning and social organizations?

Activities to Explore the Ideas

1. Observe a student in a variety of situations and events. Make written observations of each event using the ethnographic fieldnote practices of notemaking/notetaking. Taking time to focus on one student enables us to know that child in ways that otherwise might not have been possible. Indeed, what we thought we knew about a child might change significantly once we've had a chance to engage in close observation. How did your perceptions of your student change through the process of descriptive review?
2. Focusing on one child at a time is invaluable but also difficult in the rush of classroom activities. What structures might you build into your daily routine that would enable you to periodically focus on one child for a given period of time?
3. Analyze the observations using the headings described in this book, or create headings of your own. Compare and contrast the student's participation in different events. Have you supported your interpretations with evidence from your fieldnotes?

Suggested Readings

Kanevsky, R. 1993. "Descriptive Review of a Child: A Way of Knowing About Teaching and Learning." In *Inside-Outside: Teacher Research and Knowledge,* edited by M. Cochran-Smith and S. Lytle. New York: Columbia University.

Dyson, A. H. 1995. "Children Out of Bounds: The Power of Case Studies in Expanding Visions of Literacy Development." In *A Handbook for Literacy Educators: Research on Teaching the Communicative and Visual Arts,* edited by J. Flood, S. B. Heath, and D. Lapp.

Anne Haas Dyson is an expert at observing young children, especially when writing. This chapter will lead you to her other wonderful books.

Almy, M., and C. Genishi. 1975. *Ways of Studying Children: An Observation Manual for Early Childhood Teachers.*

A seminal work for teachers and parents who want to know more about observing young children.

6

Reflective Practice Through Ethnography

Josh, one of the student teachers, wrote to his cooperating teacher in a journal that they kept in the classroom. He wrote about finishing up a lesson. His cooperating teacher responded:

> I am continually reminded in my career of how important it is to give kids time to mull things over, then to give them time to reflect and have closure on the things they've learned. Then these things can be used like Velcro to attach future learnings to. I learned also through a science project I was involved in—without the reflection part, I often remained confused as to what I learned from an experiment.

Merely reflecting on our teaching is not enough. In order for that reflection to affect practice, teachers and student teachers need to engage in discussions with others about their reflections. They need opportunities for dialoguing to generate options for changing their practice. Building on the ideas of Judith Green and Carol Dixon (1999), I explore the differences between "reflection" and "reflexivity" and discuss a theoretical frame for studying reflective practice. In addition, I categorize the kinds of reflections these student teachers wrote and discover how they made use of this reflective practice.

Reflective Practice and Students as Learners

How does reflection lead to learning? Marshall (1992) has created two metaphors for teaching. In the first metaphor (students as workers), students are seen as passive recipients and producers of products. Memorizing facts is important as is extrinsic motivation and correctness. In the second metaphor (students as learners), students learn the processes of learning, becoming thinkers who learn from mistakes and errors and use their knowledge of learning in other situations. Instead of just memorizing facts, students use problem solving to understand complex relationships.

Firestone (1992) builds on this work of classroom metaphors and discusses how the metaphor of student as learner is more in line with the research paradigms that look at student-centered classrooms. In this research paradigm, not only is the student seen as a learner, but the teacher is also seen as a learner. He describes teachers in these kinds of classrooms as being "problem solvers who plan, assess, and adjust" (268) their practices based on their knowledge of their students and based on their knowledge of the craft of teaching and learning. Firestone states:

> This new paradigm highlighted (uncertainty). In effect it made teachers learners in complex settings and suggested that teachers were supposed to use a wide array of teaching strategies to make learners out of students as well. . . .
>
> Teaching is viewed as uncertain by those who believe teachers must significantly adjust their approaches to reflect subject matter, students, and other contingencies. The *reflective practice paradigm*, with its emphasis on the range of factors teachers must consider and the complexity of problem solving required, highlights uncertainty. (269)

From this perspective, reflective practice makes teachers problem solvers who are constantly adjusting their practice depending on their subject and their students. Because teachers have a new group of students each year, constant adjusting and finding solutions to problems is what teachers do. It is why teachers are constantly learning from new situations. As a teacher of teachers, I wanted to help new teachers develop strategies for problem solving that they could use for a range of problems depending on their situations. I decided to search for examples of problems in the student teachers' reflection journals. I discovered that just as they had many different *uses* for reflection (Figure 6–1), they also had many *types* of reflections (Figure 6–2).

Student Teachers Reflecting on Practice

As I looked through all the student teachers' reflections, I discovered that they used them for a variety of purposes: 1) to change what was not working; 2) to think through actions; 3) to relieve frustration; 4) to connect the theories of learning with the practice of instruction; and 5) to examine their own teaching expertise (Figure 6–1).

I also categorized the types of reflections that the student teachers wrote (Figure 6–2) and found four kinds of journal reflections: 1) journaling with

Use	Example
To change practice	Mary and Maria changing lessons
To think through actions	Aurora's bed-to-bed reflection
To relieve frustration	Maria wanting to work at McDonalds
To connect theory and practice	Mary and the Directed Listening Thinking Activity lesson
To examine their own teaching expertise	Credential portfolio reflections

Figure 6–1. *Uses for Reflection*

Journal	Audience	Reflection
Cooperating Teacher and Student Teacher	Cooperating Teacher and Student Teacher	Communicating with Cooperating Teacher, planning and getting feedback, solving problems
Supervisor and Student Teacher	Supervisor and Student Teacher	Relieving the tension problem solving, relationships
Lesson Plan Reflections	Instructor and Supervisor	Thinking through the lesson, problem solving, reacting and changing
Portfolio Reflections	Cooperating Teacher, Supervisor, and Student Teacher	Providing evidence for obtaining credential

Figure 6–2. *Types of Reflection*

their cooperating teacher; 2) journaling with me, their supervisor; 3) reflecting on lesson plans; and 4) reflecting on artifacts they were keeping for their teacher portfolio.

Cooperating Teacher Journal Reflections

One of the benefits of traditional student teaching was having someone mentor the student teachers as they were working side by side every day. By giving constant and immediate feedback about the situated practices that occurred in that particular classroom, the student teachers learned important instructional strategies and learned about the teacher thinking that demanded constant teacher decisions. The importance of this partnership between experienced mentors and apprentices was clear to me after I read a journal written between Ana and her cooperating teacher. These two teachers developed a good rapport and spoke to each other often during the day.

In looking at their journal, I found that Ana was able to reflect on and change her teaching practice because of the feedback that she received from her cooperating teacher. This teacher would watch Ana during a lesson and then generate options for her concerning any changes she thought Ana could make. This was important for Ana, who was always searching for ways to improve her practice. She positioned herself as a learner as she wrote in this journal:

> I think you have been giving me great experiences that are helping me prepare for the next step, and then the next step, etc. I really am thankful for all your input you have been giving me. Both the good and the bad are greatly appreciated. I really like to know what you are thinking. It helps me to reflect further!

In dialoging with Ana, this cooperating teacher was able to show her how some teachers think about fears and apprehensions in the culture of teaching. More importantly, she directed the focus back on the classroom students so that Ana was guided to see how teachers create student-centered classrooms. She wrote back:

> Please take my feedback not as "good/bad" but as strengths/stretches. You are a good teacher/person with many strengths/stretches. . . . As am I. By the way—my fears have not yet vanished, and I am still not completely comfortable. I am less nervous all the time, and more confident as I gain experiences. I think many teachers might confess the same. I worry now that students may not learn and grow as much as they should. What if they can't fluently read? What if they don't understand primary math concepts? I'm nervous that I might say something that would make students feel insecure or hinder their success. I will always be fearful that my Spanish fluency will somehow prevent instead of promote language development. Yet, somehow I have faith—in my values, principles, understandings, and commitments to each child I know.

When Ana wrote that she "panicked when it was time to dismiss the children" and wanted to "steal" her cooperating teacher's idea of dismissing the students by the color of their shirts, Ana's teacher wrote back:

> With regards to dismissal—"steal" all ideas. It's not "stealing." It's sharing. I'm the teacher I am because of the teachers who share with me. I appreci-

ate the way you approached Rosa with the plastic bag, and how you taught Alejandro about the date. Let your teacher shine through!

In this response, Ana's cooperating teacher directed the reflection to emphasize classroom students and teaching practices.

Supervisor Journal Reflections

The student teachers also wrote a journal for me, their supervisor. I found that this journal had a range of uses. Often this journal was just a place for them to alleviate tension. For example, at the end of this long, difficult year, when she almost had her teaching credential, Maria wrote:

> Well . . . today I had one of those days that makes me want to give up and work at McDonalds!

Other times the student teachers wrote about personal difficulties, fights with boyfriends, problems with instructors, small disagreements with cooperating teachers or other teachers in our school. They did not want answers to these problems, only a place to let off steam.

They also used the journal to think back on instructional practice and on the things they were observing in their placements. By writing down the exemplary teaching strategies that they observed, they discovered what kinds of things were important for teachers at different grade levels and how children developed differently. For instance, Mary wrote early in the fall during the beginning of this student teaching year:

> First grade is like another world. I see how clear and detailed instructions must be, and how slow you must speak in order for the kids to understand. I have also learned that things must be made fun and interesting in order for the kids to stay focused. They must have their assignments modeled to them because they learn very visually.

Bed-to-Bed Reflections

In the lesson plan reflections some of the student teachers talked through their lessons as a way of thinking about what had happened. For example, Aurora wrote a reflection on the first day she taught a language arts lesson to her sixth grade class. Her reflection is a good example of what Graves calls a "bed-to-bed story" (1983, 156). He writes that, "In warming to my subject, I often write a three paragraph lead or even three to four pages before I grasp a subject." Since these student teachers were not writing stories for publication but were using their writing to think through the difficult and complex issues of teaching and learning in classrooms, their bed-to-bed reflections served them well. By listing all the actions that she had attended to, Aurora was "warming to her subject" and gaining a newer understanding of what she was doing, why, and whether or not she would do it again. She wrote:

> Before the students came in this morning, I wrote an agenda on the board for the students to see what we were going to cover during this period of time. I thought that there would be some students who preferred to see what we were going to do, and I also thought it would be helpful for me to glance at. Actually, I didn't end up using it because I was using my written lesson plan schedule that I had on the table in front of me. I also forgot to mention it to the students, so I'm not sure how many students even noticed it being there. I do think that putting the agenda on the board is a good idea though, so I plan on putting an agenda on the board again tomorrow and will mention why it's there to the kids. That way, as soon as they get settled, we can go over what is expected during the language arts time.

Shifting of Action—Taking New Action

Student teachers used lesson plan reflections in two other important ways. In the following two examples, first Mary reflected on how she would change the way she did a lesson in the future, and Maria reflected on how she changed what she did with a lesson *in the moment*. These two uses of lesson plan reflections seemed to bring meaning to the idea of "reflective practice" in which the student teachers did not just think about what happened but actually took action based on their reflections.

In the first example, Mary taught a DLTA lesson (Directed Listening Thinking Activity [Stauffer 1975]) in which students in her first grade classroom made predictions and gave evidence from the text. As all teachers who have used this powerful strategy are aware, when some students are familiar with the book, the activity does not always go as planned. Mary wrote that, "before I taught it, I tried to have everything planned out to a tee, so it would go as well as I pictured." However, she discovered early that the lesson planned is not always the lesson implemented:

> The first problem I had was that many of the students had already read the book I chose to use. That made things a bit difficult, especially since the lesson was about making predictions. They already knew what the story was about so, consequently, their predictions were correct. Even though I already knew this, for the sake of the other kids who had not heard of this book yet, I treated their

predictions as I had originally planned. I still asked them at different parts of the book if they wanted to change their predictions, and whether or not they had evidence from the book to support their predictions. This way the lesson wasn't really completely ruined. Nonetheless, I realized too late that I should have picked a different, perhaps less common, book for this lesson.

At this point in Mary's reflection, she was thinking back on what had happened and what changes she "should have" made. She had not initiated any changes. However, this lesson was taught to a small group during a round robin grouping system, and she was about to teach it to three more groups. Mary writes how she modified the lesson for subsequent groups:

With the other groups, I was a little more prepared. As soon as I showed them the cover of the book and some said they had it at home, I asked them to please not tell their friends what it was about because it would ruin the surprise for them. *Most* of them respected that, but a few had some problems holding it in. . . . Next time I definitely know to be more aware of how common the book I choose is for the age group I am teaching because it can put a major dent in the lesson.

Mary's reflection illustrated how she made it clear to herself why she had problems with DLTA at this particular time and how she would remedy it the next time she taught this lesson. In the next example, Maria's reflection shows how she made adjustments in her lesson on a moment-by moment basis.

Maria was teaching in a bilingual first grade classroom in the fall during *El Día de Los Muertos* (a Mexican holiday, The Day of the Dead, celebrated during fall). She arranged for the students to visit a parents' house where there was an altar for the holiday. After that the students returned to the classroom and Maria began a lesson in which she was going to have them learn about basic story structure (beginning, middle, and end) by writing a story containing these elements. In her reflection, Maria wrote that, "From this lesson I learned much about modifications." She expected that the students would eagerly begin writing and instead found that they began by drawing pictures. She thought they were doing a prewrite activity but discovered that they were just drawing. She writes how she modified the lesson:

At that moment I decided to stop the activity and ask each student individually what we were doing. Some responded that they were writing about Halloween or *Día de Los Muertos*; others just looked at me, fiddling with their crayons in their hands.

I had to ask myself, what was more important for the students. . . . Instead of having them write stories in which they had a beginning, middle, and end, I asked them to reflect on the field trip.

I recognize that the outcome of my lesson differs significantly from my objectives. However, I feel that I learned so much from this experience that I cannot regret it. . . . I cannot say that this lesson was a failure because, by tailoring the lesson for their needs, I got to serve them better. For example, instead of having them write a story and point out the beginning, middle, and conclusion, they were able to verbally recognize those three elements of the story. What is more important is that we all had a good time going about this process.

Once I got off my trip (of having to execute my lesson exactly as planned), I was able to enjoy the learning process with my students. We sat around talking about all the different things we saw on the altar, other experiences, and family members who had passed away.

Both of these examples show how student teachers used the lesson plan reflections to solve problems and find solutions. In Mary's case, she realized that when teaching comprehension through a DLTA lesson, problems arise when students are familar with the text. In her reflection, she generated different options of what to do in the moment and what she might do the next time she taught this lesson.

Maria's reflection explored how closely teachers must stay with their planned lessons. When we adapt the lesson to follow the students' interest in the moment, do we sacrifice the content and our objectives or do we begin to get closer to student-centered classrooms? Maria's reflection shows a respect for the learner, a desire to join the learners herself. If we always know exactly where we are headed with our lesson plans and always know what objectives we must meet, then we might miss surprises along the way? We might miss opportunities for learning because we are so tuned in to the lesson instead of being tuned in to the students and the subject.

Portfolio Reflections

Two times during the year the student teachers discussed their credential portfolio with me (their supervisor) and with the cooperating teachers. This collection of artifacts gave the new teachers a way of looking at themselves as lifelong learners (as ethnographers) and a way of looking at their teaching as social practice (social and cultural practices of a group). This ethnographic practice of artifact analysis (examining the objects they had collected over the year) gave teachers a method or tool for understanding their classrooms as cultures. Members used artifacts in their everyday lives to become particular kinds of members of certain types of cultures. In this case, student teachers were collecting and reflecting on the artifacts of classrooms in order to join the culture of teaching. This portfolio was a way of looking at and reflecting on the differences and changes in themselves that came about during this year of student teaching. It was also a vehicle for continuing in the role of learner throughout their teaching careers.

The portfolios were structured so that the student teachers collected artifacts for the six domains of teaching. These domains guided their selection process throughout the year so that their reflections were purposeful. In California, the teaching certificate standards include these six domains:

1. Teachers will create and maintain an effective environment for student learning.
2. Teachers will understand and organize subject matter for student learning.
3. Teachers will plan instruction and design learning experiences for all students.
4. Teachers will engage all students in powerful learning.
5. Teachers will assess student learning.
6. Teachers will develop as professional educators to improve teaching and learning.

"Next time, I would just push desks and chairs out of the way."

Most of the student teachers used their classroom map assignment to show that they could create and maintain an effective environment for student learning. However, Aurora discussed how she learned that the environment can be negotiated every day depending on the needs of the students and depending on what is being taught. For example, she was teaching a language arts unit on myths one day and having the sixth graders work with sequencing sentence strips. The room was not large, and there were many students and many desks. However, Aurora writes on her reflection of this activity:

> I think that part of the problem was the setting of this project. I was using the linoleum portion of the room to lay out the strips and this was the area the kids were "squeezed" into to recreate the story. I should have had them in a large circle. I think this would have worked better. I used the space that was available, rather than think about creating a space in the room for this purpose. Next time, I would just push desks and chairs out of the way and create a space large enough for a large circle.

"I'm questioning whether they understand the math but just don't understand the language."

One of the student teachers in this group was born in Cambodia and came to the United States when she was very young. During this year of student teaching, she sometimes struggled to find the correct terminology. She was multilingual and could read and write in several languages. When she taught math lessons, she sometimes found that the math terminology needed to be exact for her bilingual (in Spanish) sixth graders. One day she told me that there were so many types of math concepts and math-related language to be learned. In one of the lessons, she said "sum up" instead of "find the sum of." In her reflection she showed how she used her knowledge of languages as a resource to look from the child's perspective. She wrote:

> I'm finding that a lot of the problems that the students have involving math is tied to language. For example some of the students would not know what to do if this was the direction: Find the fifth letter in NUMBER. What I'm questioning now about the students is whether they understand the math but just don't understand the language.

"Planning, I thought, was inhuman."

Coming from a different culture and language made the transition into the culture of teachers of the United States more difficult for Sue. She once wrote in a reflection about how important planning was to her now as a teacher:

> Everything needs to be written down and scheduled. When I was little my parents used to joke about how Americans run around with a plan book in their hands. I used to think that planning was what crazy people did. Planning, I thought, was inhuman. Planning is probably the most important thing in my life today.

When Sue taught a lesson in her sixth grade classroom on the "Problem of the Day" in math, she solved the problem of planning the structuring of the lesson. She wrote about how she would change it the next time:

> I took *way* too long talking. When I did this, I lost them. I will try to avoid having to make long explanations when I teach. I just didn't know how to turn the explaining responsibility to the students. I couldn't do that either because the way I structured my lesson did not allow it. I did not create an atmosphere of participation. If I were one of the students, I wouldn't

volunteer to explain either because I had no obligation. If I had assigned a reporter from each group to report a solution, I would have created that obligation.

In this reflection, we see a student teacher looking for problems, not in the students, but in the way that the lesson was structured. She realized that she wanted to be a teacher who planned instruction so that students take on the responsibility for participating in the lessons and so that they become the learners, the owners of the task. Sue also shows in this reflection that she is adept at watching her students and looking at the lessons from their perspective.

Engaging Students

It was wonderful to see the student teachers drawing from their own resources to engage their students. For example, Maria's first graders put on a play during her first takeover in the fall because she had been in theater herself and enjoyed acting. Sue showed off her many diaries to her kindergartners when she wanted them to begin writing in journals. Josh was an expert at physical education and created new games with his students. Aurora was once a librarian and did a unit on Dr. Seuss which included a timeline of his books. Alice was a landscape architect and showed her sixth graders how to plot and draw plans for houses. Helen had taught in Japan for three years and engaged her students in Japanese literature. Lydia developed a unit on community. She used her knowledge of community work and her membership in the Multicultural Community Outreach Program as a Latino Program Coordinator to enable her students to learn about interdependence. With Ana's knowledge of Spanish from a variety of perspectives and cultures, she was able to provide Spanish instruction to her students. Mary was Irish and pulled from her experiences to engage her students. She writes:

> I taught a St. Patrick's Day lesson during language arts last week. It went really well. I brought in some Irish soda bread, my old Irish step dancing costume from when I was little, my claddaugh ring, a clip from the *Riverdance* movie, and a book about St. Patrick's Day. I then had them do some creative writing about a leprechaun who lost his pot of gold. The stories turned out so cute!

"How can a test tell you everything?"

Helen was an English teacher for three years in Japan before she entered our teacher education program. She used her experiences in Japan to amplify her practices as a teacher. In the reflection that she wrote for her portfolio, she compared the two cultural styles of teaching:

> I entered this program thinking the only way for true assessment is the way the Japanese have done it for decades, a test. Boy was I not with the changing times. Test? Assessing student learning can be done through so many more meaningful channels. . . . Students come with so many learning styles and talents, how can a test tell you everything? There has been so much growth here with portfolios and informal assessments.

Transcription: Professional Educators Improving Practice

In addition to writing reflections, each student teacher was asked by the teacher education program at this university to do an audiotape of one of their lessons, and after listening to the tape, to answer questions about it. The goal of this assignment was to help student teachers focus on the importance of conversations in the classroom (Green 1983). Then they were asked to turn in an analysis of the audiotape concerning such things as:

1. How many questions did you ask, and what kind were they (knowledge, comprehension, application, evaluation)?
2. Did you state the academic and social expectations for your students?
3. Was your use of language explicit and developmentally appropriate?
4. What might you do differently next time?

Because I was interested in using an ethnographic approach with these student teachers, I also required my small group of nine student teachers to do a short "transcription" of the audiotape. I explained a little about sociolinguistic and discourse analysis and showed them how to listen to a portion of the tape and write down every word that was spoken and to indicate *how* it was spoken. For example, if the speaker spoke in a loud voice, the transcriber might put the words in capitals.

The practice of listening to the words of the classroom was not automatic with the student teachers. After listening to a friend talk about how "transcription" had helped her reading clinic teachers change their teaching practice (Cruse 1995), I thought this practice might also help to slow down the action for these student teachers so that they could actually "see" what was being said.

For one of the student teachers, Sue, the assignment helped her reflect on her classroom practices and change her teaching. The lesson that she audiotaped and transcribed was about "desert scenery" in preparation for a book her kindergartners were about to read. Sue found that her words became a diversion instead of a path to the intended instructional goal. Her transcript of the desert event in kindergarten is below:

Sue: Mmmmm. I can't believe we have only twenty-one days left of school. That is scary. I am really going to miss you guys. You're the best class I have ever had.

Student: Why are you going back to the sixth grade?

Sue: I am not going back to the sixth grade. I am not going to be at Island View anymore. I am going back home to Los Angeles.

Students: Ahhhhh.

Sue: I am really going to miss you.

Student A: You're not going to be a teacher?

Student B: I am going to miss you.

Sue: I am going to be a teacher, not here, but in Los Angeles.

Student C: Why don't you go teach in Brazil?

Student D: Hey, I can go visit you during the summer because my uncle lives that way.

Sue: One question at a time. If you'd like me to answer your questions, we're going to have to take turns talking. I can't go teach in Brazil because I would not have a license to teach there, and I don't speak the language. But anyhow, today I am going to read to you a story and it's called, *Welcome to the Sea of Sand.* Before I read this story, I would like, ummm, one person at a time to tell me about, to describe the kind of place where this story is happening. Mmmmm. What kinds of things might you find here?

Sue realized that she had started the instructional lesson with a conversation about what she was going to do at the end of the school year. The students listened to what she first began talking to them about and started thinking about where she would be teaching. They were reading her as a text, listening to the words she spoke, reacting to those words, making inferences and predictions, just as they would have done with a text (Green and Dixon 1993). Sue had been diverted from her lesson objectives by her own words when what she had wanted instead was a good "anticipatory set" or focusing topic for her lesson. However, the important part of this audiotape/transcription activity for Sue was the discovery and reflection she did afterward about her teaching practice and the changes that she would make the next time. Sue writes about the transcript:

First of all, the end of the school year was in the air so I began by talking with the children about how there were only twenty-one days of school left.

I believe I didn't lead the discussion into the right direction. We ended up talking about my move back home to Los Angeles. I got to a place where I did not know how to get back on track with the lesson I was supposed to present, which was about desert scenery. Perhaps I should have told the children that Los Angeles is pretty much a desert; then I could have been able to make a connection. As a teacher, should I be careful about going off on a tangent sometimes?

For Sue, being able to look at her words on paper slowed down the instructional and interactional process so that she could see and understand what she wanted to change or keep in her teaching practice. She writes, "There are all these errors that I am catching. But I think I am getting it. I can identify the problem and then work with it." Sometimes the task of teaching can be so overwhelming that beginners miss the details. The details are what gives the craft of teaching its energy and strength. An ethnographic perspective helped Sue realize the importance of the words that teachers say.

This reflection suggests two other points. First, by writing to an audience, her supervisor, Sue was engaging in a discussion about her practice. This is the difference between just writing a reflection and discussing that reflection with someone in order to generate options about what could be changed. Sue writes: "Perhaps I should have told the children that Los Angeles is pretty much a desert; then I could have been able to make a connection." By dialoguing with another person about her practice, she was able to think of other ways of teaching. Second, this reflection shows that the teacher was not afraid of examining the parts of her practice that did not measure up to her expectations. She was willing to analyze the "talk" on the transcript and make suggestions about what might have been. In this way, this student teacher was using an ethnographic approach, becoming a learner, taking risks, and making the most of her chance to talk to others about what she was doing in the classroom.

Summary

One of the most useful reflections was when these student teachers reflected on why they had entered the teaching profession now that they had such an insider's view of the culture of teaching. If the students could remember their first sudden "leaps to judgment" and then reflect back on that from the perspective of a practicing teacher, they gained an appreciation for struggles that teachers face. For example, in the fall and during her first placement Maria was plagued with ideas of how to change education and especially how to make it better for Latinos. At first, instead of looking from the perspective of her cooperating teacher, she tried to make changes in the classroom based on her ideals and personal opinions. She was confused and exasperated because many of the things that she tried did not enact the changes that she wanted. However, during the end of her second placement, Maria again showed her exasperation but this time from the perspective of a teacher. In this journal reflection, Maria parallels some of the concerns for students voiced by Ana's cooperating teacher:

> I hate making excuses, rationalizing my utter failures but we did have rehearsal, Culture Fair, field trips, moving, star testing. Despite all of these changes in our program I still question my effectiveness as a teacher especially because my teaching is not in my dominate language. A part of me asks myself why I do this to myself—twice as much work: translating lessons, dittos, bilingual texts. I wonder if I had chosen to teach in a monolingual English classroom if things would be easier. (My cooperating teacher) is great, she continues to support me and stresses that we have a challenging classroom. But I can't help wondering if my lesson failures are attributed to my lack of Spanish academic acquisition. Maybe I am the reason why my students don't understand "time." I just feel so frustrated because most of the time I am spending trying to get the students to just follow directions. I can't deal with creating and modifying curriculum to fit the needs of all my students—It's crazy!! I have students who cannot draw a clock to students who can answer time questions. I don't know . . . I really can't see myself not teaching bilingual/bicultural students, they're the reason I got into teaching in the first place.

Further Inquiry into Ideas

1. Are there other ways of reflecting on practice besides writing reflections?

2. What is it about the *writing* of reflections that makes them more valuable?

3. What kinds of metaphors come to mind when you think about teaching and learning? Can you draw a picture of teaching and learning?

Activities to Explore the Ideas

1. Set up a camera or a tape recorder and videotape or audiotape your classroom during a particular event. Then look or listen to the tape and decide which part you want to transcribe. Examine the transcript in order to see your words and the words of your students written on paper. What questions do you want to ask yourself about the classroom talk?

What would you change the next time you taught this lesson? Share this videotape or audiotape with your students for their reactions.

2. Begin a dialogue journal with another teacher in your school. Do you begin to think about changes you can make in your practice depending on what you write?

3. Begin a dialogue journal with other student teachers. Are the problems you are having similar? What strategies are you building to solve these problems?

Suggested Readings

Marshall, H. H., ed. 1992. *Redefining Student Learning: Roots of Educational Change.* Norwood, NJ: Ablex.
This book is a collection of articles from an ethnographic and sociolinguistic perspective focused on learning in classrooms.

Atkinson, P. 1990. *The Ethnographic Imagination: Textual Constructions of Reality.* London: Routledge.
If you are as interested in ethnography as I am, you may enjoy reading how our fieldnotes of the events are only constructions that we create and not the actual events as they happened. In this book, Paul Atkinson describes the different ethnographic accounts as different kinds of texts.

Jennings, L. 1998. "Teachers View Learning Through Ethnographic Eyes: Lessons from a Summer Institute." *California Reader* 31 (4): 11–15.
In this article, Louise Jennings, a member of the Santa Barbara Classroom Discourse Group, reflects on how members of the South Coast Writing Group used ethnography to observe their own summer institute.

Wallat, C., J. L. Green, S. Conlin, and M. Haramis. 1983. "Issues Related to Action Research in the Classroom: The Teacher and Researcher as a Team." In *Ethnography and Language in Educational Settings,* edited by J. L. Green and C. Wallat, 87–113. Norwood, NJ: Ablex.

7

Classroom Observations

Alice, one of the student teachers, reflected on ethnography and classroom observations:

> I believe there were many benefits to this process of learning to see with the eyes of the ethnographer. It gave me tools or a method of evaluating a new environment in order to gain access to a new community. Standing back and analyzing a community in this way is probably more important with a community you are familiar with such as a classroom. (We have all been students in similar situations.) Why? It's probably easier to analyze a community which is very foreign to the observer because your level of understanding is low to begin with. In familiar environments it's easy to miss a lot of the "hidden" or "invisible" messages embedded within the physical layout or the discourse between community members because it's too familiar.

In this chapter I explore some answers to the first question of this book, how ethnography can help student teachers (and also infrequent visitors to classrooms such as principals, supervisors, parents) become better classroom observers. Student teachers need guidelines on: how to observe classrooms, what to observe, from which perspective to observe, for what purpose they are observed, and what kind of language they will use. We assume that to tell them to "observe" is enough. Over thirty years ago, Karl Popper wrote that observation needed to be selective, with a definite purpose, a problem, a point of view, and a language:

> Twenty-five years ago I tried to bring home the same point to a group of physics students in Vienna by beginning a lecture with the following instructions: "Take pencil and paper; carefully observe, and write down what you have observed!" They asked, of course, what I wanted them to observe.

Clearly the instruction "Observe!" is absurd. (It is not even idiomatic, unless the object of the transitive verb can be taken as understood.) Observation is always selective. It needs a chosen object, a definite task, an interest, a point of view, a problem. And its description presupposes a descriptive language, with property words; it presupposes similarity and classification, which in its turn presupposes interest, points of view, and problems. (Popper 1963, 21, as cited in Evertson and Green 1986)

The ethnographic tools that these nine student teachers used gave them a systematic way of observing classrooms with guidelines about what events to observe, how to see from a member's perspective, how to take fieldnotes, how to think about point of view, and how to describe using the language of the classroom.

There were two problems that I wanted the student teachers to understand as they entered classrooms. The first one was that because of their familiarity with classrooms, being raised mostly in schools in the United States, they would have difficulty understanding what they were seeing. They would assume that they understood the generic when it was the specific that gave classrooms their identity. The other problem that I foresaw was that they had to enter classrooms and observe for a few minutes and then write summaries based on this one-time look. I did not think that these beginning teachers would be able to interpret what was going on inside experienced teacher's classrooms, especially in just one short visit. I wanted to impress on them what I had learned as a teacher and what I had experienced as a classroom researcher in The Santa Barbara Classroom Discourse Group: It is difficult to understand what is going on inside a classroom with just one visit.

In order to make these problems meaningful to the student teachers, I told them the story of how I entered Lois Brandts' first grade classroom to do my research in the fall of 1996 after teaching first grade for ten years. I saw in the corner of her room, the same *Chicken Soup with Rice* chart that I had used with my students. I saw the same pictures of dinosaurs and reptiles on the walls. I saw math manipulatives and writing paper that was the same as I had used. I sat down with my camera and my notebook and thought, "I know all this. Why am I here?" It took me two years of observing and another year of analyzing to really understand what was going on in her classroom and to realize that it was nothing like my first grade classroom.

In addition to telling the student teachers my story, I read them a story by George and Louise Spindler (1982). These two anthropologists had written about observing and researching a familiar setting and the difficulties involved. The story begins with George telling about his ethnographies of the Menominee, the Kanai (the Blood Indians of Alberta, Canada), and the

Mistassini Cree hunters (near James Bay, Quebec). When he began doing ethnographies of elementary schools in the United States, he discovered that describing a familiar setting was more difficult than describing a strange setting. He writes:

> Making the strange familiar was not the problem in doing ethnography in schools in the u.s.a. When I (George Spindler) started fieldwork in 1950 in West Coast elementary schools, what I observed was indeed strange enough, but since it was a mirror of my own cultural strangeness I could not see it—at first. I came very near to quitting fieldwork on my first research assignment for the team I had been hired to participate in, working out of Stanford University under the direction of Robert Bush, Professor of Education. I sat in classes for days wondering what there was to "observe." Teachers taught, reprimanded, rewarded, while pupils sat at desks, squirming, whispering, reading, writing, staring into space, as they had in my own grade-school experience, in my practice teaching in a teacher training program, and in the two years of public school teaching I had done before World War II. What should I write down in my empty notebook? In the fieldwork with the Menominee, with whom we had already spent three seasons, I couldn't write fast enough or long enough, and I spent hours each night working on my field notes. And when I could take pictures I took hundreds. It never occurred to me to take a picture in any of the classrooms I worked in during the 1950s, and for several weeks in the first classrooms my notebook remained virtually empty, except for some generalized comments such as "79.1 T (we used codes for everybody) seems nervous today" or "3 girls whisper together until teacher glances in their direction and says 'Must you do that?'" The familiar was all too familiar. (23–24)

I read this story to the student teachers at the beginning of the year in order to help them understand how difficult it was going to be for them to "see" and understand what they were going to "observe" from just a quick look into the kinds of classrooms where they had been educated. I wanted them to understand that to enter a class at one point in time or to select one event to study may be problematic if the goal is to understand what students have an opportunity to learn in individual classrooms (The Santa Barbara Classroom Discourse Group 1992b).

A Mirror of Our Own Cultural Strangeness

The assignment from the teacher education program for these student teachers was to visit four classrooms each semester and observe and then write up

1. What was the purpose of the lesson?
2. How was the lesson opened?
3. What were the basic steps to the lesson?
4. How was the lesson ended?
5. Describe the class rules and management techniques you observed.
6. Additional comments on interesting things you were able to observe: e.g., classroom environment, student interactions.

Figure 7–1. *Format for Classroom Observation Notes*

a summary of each observation. The student teachers were asked to use their experiences with notetaking/notemaking to gather fieldnotes. The assignment sheet in their student handbook (Figure 7–1) was meant to guide them through this process.

Although this guide was meant to help them do the assignment, it was difficult for me to ask the nine student teachers in my small group to follow it since it was not grounded in an ethnographic frame and came from another perspective entirely. Instead, I gave them another set of questions (Figure 7–2) to use in their observations of classrooms taken from an article written by the Santa Barbara Classroom Discourse Group from the *Journal of Classroom Interaction* ("Do you see what we see? The referential and intertextual nature of classroom life," [1992b]).

- From whose perspective will we view this life?
- What is the appropriate amount of time needed to understand life as members do?
- What events are occurring?
- When did the event begin, and when will it end?
- What is required to be a member of this group and to participate in socially and academically appropriate ways?
- What can we see if we enter the classroom at a particular point in time?
- What evidence do we need to support the claims we wish to make about learning in any given class?
- What are the consequences for members living in a particular classroom?

Figure 7–2. *Observing Ongoing Life in Classrooms*

I wanted them to know, from a teacher's perspective, that they would be entering as strangers into a community that had been built up over a long period of time; one that had constructed particular ways of being teachers, students, and learners. They would be entering an ongoing stream of activity, crossing the river in the middle. They could look down from a bridge and watch the water rushing by but in no way would they be able to really understand what was happening unless they jumped in and swam down the river with this group. Even then, they would be missing events at the source. I knew that if they could understand this view, then it would help them with their first placement as they observed how the classroom culture was being constructed. It would also help them in their second placement when they would have to jump in midstream.

When observing these classrooms from an ethnographic perspective, I showed them how they might look at two aspects of classroom life (space and time) and the questions they might ask (Figure 7–3). In developing this guide for them, I was drawing on Spradley (1980), Erickson (1982), and on an article written by Susan Florio-Ruane (1990), a teacher educator from Michigan State University.

Observation is not passive. Observers look, listen, ask, record, and analyze. Tools of the trade: a notebook, a pencil, and perhaps audiotape and videotape recorders.

Looking at Space

Classroom maps
What is space used for?
What activities occur in which spaces?
Who can go where? When? Why?
What are the social and academic spaces?

Looking at Time

Event maps
Log the activities (or the events) of the hour, day, week, year.
How do the students identify chunks of time?
What is scheduled? What is the real schedule?
What does the plan book say? Does it happen?

Figure 7–3. *Classroom Observation*

Before and After

The nine student teachers turned in their four observation summaries of four classes at the end of the first semester. In some cases, because they had not received feedback from me, the students had made interpretations that I did not think were supported by evidence. For example, some students wrote things like: "She has a lot of respect for her students," or "Management didn't seem like an issue at all," without giving any detailed information to accompany their evaluations. I was constantly writing, "Where is your evidence?" on their papers. This problem could have been solved by having the students turn in the observations one at a time and getting feedback with each observation.

However, in the second semester, the student teachers began to use their "ethnographic eyes" (Jennings 1998) to make interpretations based on evidence. For example, in this summary of a classroom observation, Sue shows how she learned that she needs to give evidence for her judgments:

> There may be another way to look at this classroom. It might be small, but if we look at it from being one station (center) in a whole big classroom (the whole preschool), the space is indeed appropriate. As I had said earlier, perhaps this classroom area is reserved for academic use. When it is playtime, the children might be able to go play in another area of the preschool. (I should have asked Janet about this. Questions like this always come up when you start reflecting and because you don't think of them during the time that you're there, you end up having to make up hypotheses.) There is, however, evidence that the tiny classroom is only one "station" of the whole preschool. For example, when we went to watch a video on counting, we went into the chapel and watched the video with another class. As we were walking down the hall to the chapel, I noticed other small classrooms, like (the teacher's).

The student teachers also showed in the second semester that they were looking for the less obvious patterns and the implicit routines in the classroom. This is what Spradley (1972) called "ideational order" of the culture. For example, Maria shows in this sample of her classroom observations how she is using her ethnographic perspective to ask the questions: who can do or say what, when, under what circumstances, for what purpose, with what outcomes. After writing her descriptive, noninterpretive fieldnotes, she analyzed the notes to understand the classroom in more depth. Maria observed a bilingual third grade where the language of instruction was Spanish and none of the students had transitioned into English instruction. She writes:

> I observed her (the teacher) talking with the Teaching Assistant in English. I wonder if they speak together in English for efficiency or what. I also won-

der if when the adults speak in English they are giving students the message that the language of adults is English while the language of students is Spanish.

In an interview with the cooperating teacher, we learned that speaking in English to other adults in the room in her bilingual (in Spanish) classroom has been an issue for many years. In fact, this teacher explained to us that the children in the room, always the best ethnographers, asked her why this happens. The student teacher and the cooperating teacher therefore tried to talk to each other in Spanish as much as was possible.

Classroom Observations for Supervisors

As a supervisor of student teachers, I now use my knowledge of ethnographic fieldnotes to observe student teachers. Because I write down as much of the talk of the classroom and actions of the participants as I can, I use my descriptive fieldnotes as the basis for discussions with the student teacher. I can say to the student teacher, "Here is what happened. Tell me what was going on here." In this respect, I am joining a group of educational ethnographers who are finding multiple uses for ethnography in education (Egan-Robertson and Bloome 1998; Heath 1983; Sunsteen and Green 1944; Yeager, Floriani, and Green 1998).

In this section, I refer to the work of Deborah Smith (Green 1983), a supervisor who found many of the constructs of ethnography to be of value to her student teachers. For instance, when considering the participation rules of the classroom, Smith found that:

> Participation rules offered the most difficulty for student (teachers). They seemed to expect that children would continue following the same ground rules that the cooperating teacher had established, no matter who was teaching, and thus rarely stated any rules for their own lessons. Children initially spent a good deal of time testing the old rules, in order to establish, through interactional sequences, whether this context was, in fact, the same as their usual classroom context. From the student teachers' frame of reference, this behavior was an affront, rather than an active attempt to infer rules. In the first 4 days in the classroom, 16 of the 19 of my written comments on the students' teaching concerned the lack of clear rules for participation in lessons. (230)

Student teachers often begin their lessons without establishing the ground rules for participation, expecting that the students will act the same as they do for their cooperating teacher. One exception was when I was observing Aurora teach a small reading group during a language arts period. In this lesson, Aurora laid out clearly for the sixth graders exactly what she expected from them:

> I want everyone to follow along with the reader. These are some ways I will know you are following along: If you are looking at the passage being read; if you are following the words being read with your fingertip; if you're following the words being read with the eraser tip of your pencil; if you are quietly saying the words as they're being read. Also, each student needs to be following so when I call on you, you know where the previous student left off.

Not surprisingly, all of the sixth graders followed along with the oral reading in the ways that Aurora suggested. I often think that our classroom students enjoy being told exactly how they are to appropriately act and speak in different events in classrooms because that way they do not have to worry about "getting it wrong." However, instead of telling them the participation rules or generating the rules with the students, we sometimes assume they already know how to act and speak. Then we chastise them if they do not act according to the way we wanted them to participate!

The observations that I do with my current student teachers at California State University, Los Angeles, include writing ethnographic fieldnotes through notetaking/notemaking. As I observe in their classrooms, I write down as quickly as I can all the talk and actions that I see and hear within the time frame that I am observing. If I happen to see something that strikes me or that I want to remember to mention to the student teacher, I will write "PN" (personal note) in the margin and go on with my fieldnotes. In this way, my student teacher and I can "cook up" the notes together. These notes are the basis for the discussion I have with the student teacher after the observation. We go over the notes and talk about what happened in the lesson.

In this way, my job as an observer is not to jump to judgments based on one short visit into the classroom (which sometimes supervisors do because they think it is the way to help new teachers). Instead, I use myself as an *instrument of observation* and view the student teacher's classroom as descriptively as possible, writing down as much of the talk and actions as I can. Then I leave it up to the student teacher to reflect on practice as they read over my fieldnotes and discuss what is happening in the classroom from a member's perspective. Because I think there is value in sharing expertise, I put in my two-cents worth with my "PN" notes. I try to keep them positive and minimal.

In this sample of my fieldnotes as a supervisor, the student teacher, Richard, was teaching fractions to a third grade class. I wrote down as much of the talk and action as I could. This example only gives a partial glimpse and is meant to be the focus of discussion between the student teacher and myself.

12:45

Richard walks around holding up student papers that were folded correctly.

"OK now with your blue paper. . . ."

"We want to make ¼. . . ."

"How many parts, Mary?" (Mary responds: "four")

"What kind Lupe?" (Lupe responds: "equal")

Richard shows them how to fold paper into fourths.

"Show me that you have half. Then fold again. . . ."

PN: Good—you did it step by step.

"Now open it up and look what you have. . . ."

"How many sections—raise your hand please. . . ."

PN: Good—it seems as if you are very consistent in having them raise hands after you ask a question.

"Kay—eyes on me. . . ."

"In order to have a fraction?" (One student responds: "equal parts")

"I have one paper with four equal parts = ¼"

"Now you will get worksheet. . . ."

"We will go over step by step. . . ."

With these fieldnotes as a basis for discussion, the student teacher and I could go back over the event as it happened. I could then ask him to reflect on what was happening, why it happened the way it did, how it happened, and what he would change or keep the same. From this short passage, questions could be generated about the way Richard had his classroom students use pieces of folded paper, the way he stressed "equal" parts, and the way he went through the lesson step by step. By making his teaching practice explicit, we had concrete constructs that he could use in other teaching situations. For example, using hands-on materials as the students were learning about fractions, repeating the important words in the lesson ("equal parts"), and sequencing lessons were all good teaching constructs to remember.

Grand Tour Observations

If you want your observations of classrooms to be from an ethnographic perspective, you can use the suggestions of James Spradley (1979) in his book *Participant Observation*. In this book, Spradley reminds us that observation is selective. However, when we observe a social situation, such as a classroom, we may be entering with a general question, "What is going on here?" He suggests that we use the same guide that we used when we engaged in ethnographic interviews (see Chapter 3). We might start with a grand tour observation (78) and look at the different dimensions of social situations, which Spradley describes as:

1. *Space:*   the physical place or places
2. *Actor:*   the people involved
3. *Activity:* a set of related acts people do
4. *Object:*   the physical things that are present
5. *Act:*   single actions that people do
6. *Event:*   a set of related activities that people carry out
7. *Time:*   the sequencing that takes place over time
8. *Goal:*   the things people are trying to accomplish
9. *Feeling:* the emotions felt and expressed

If I used this list to analyze the sample fieldnotes that I took as a supervisor (see page 90), I could identify and name many of the different dimensions of the lesson I observed. The student teacher and I would be able to uncover many *names for things* in his classroom. These *names for things* are what Spradley calls "cultural cover terms." For example, if Richard and I talked about the different kinds of objects that were used in this lesson, we might identify pencils, papers, desks, chalkboard, and worksheets. We would use these names as a starting point to ask ourselves: What other kinds of worksheets are used in the classroom. What other kinds of papers are used in the classroom? In this way, we could uncover the different domains in this particular culture and the meanings that these domains hold for the members. We could then construct a "Spradley tree":

Skill worksheet	is a kind of	
Math worksheet	is a kind of	
Fraction ditto	is a kind of	
Phonics drillsheet	is a kind of	→ Worksheet
Grammar worksheet	is a kind of	
Map of the world fill in	is a kind of	
Color the spaces	is a kind of	

I realize that most classroom observers do not have the time it takes to observe for long periods of time as do classroom researchers using ethnography. I understand that most classroom observers do not have access to video cameras and tape recorders. However, I do suggest that in order to understand what is really going on in classrooms, we need to observe from an ethnographic perspective (see Chapter 1) and observe from the angle of vision of the members of the classroom. An ethnographic perspective allows the observer to step back and analyze the classroom from the perspective of the actors in the room.

Further Inquiry into Ideas

1. How is observing a classroom similar to the kind of observation that writers talk about? (See Calkins 1986, Chapter 2, "Rehearsal: Living the Writerly Life." Calkins writes: "Rehearsal involves living wide-awake lives—seeing, hearing, noticing, wondering." [31]

2. Why is it more difficult to observe a familiar social scene than a strange one?

3. What can we learn about a culture by just knowing how they name things?

Activities to Explore the Ideas

1. Make a list of all the social settings you might observe.

2. Follow the principal of a school around for a few days. Try to observe his working life from a principal's perspective using the tools of ethnography and your "ethnographic eyes."

3. Find a social setting that is not education related and consider doing participant observation using the practice of notetaking/notemaking. Spradley (1980) suggests that the observer practice being an outsider and an insider at the same time. He writes:

> The participant observer will experience being both insider and outsider simultaneously. Consider people playing poker. Ordinary participants are part of the game. As outsiders, they act as subjects. Hayano (1978) decided to become a participant observer in poker parlors in Gardena, California. On an average weekend, six poker parlors draw several thousand people: Hayano played many thousands of hours of poker, listened to people talk, and observed their strategies for managing the game. As an insider he shuffled cards, dealt hands, made bids, bluffed, and both won and lost hands. As an insider he felt some of the same emotions during the course of the game that the ordinary participants felt. At the same time he experienced being an outsider, one who viewed the game and himself as objects. He had the uncommon experience of being a poker player and simultaneously observing himself and others behaving as poker players. He was part of the scene, yet outside the scene. (57)

Suggested Readings

Spindler, G., and L. Spindler. 1982. "Roger Harker and Schonhausen: From Familiar to Strange and Back Again." In *Doing the Ethnography of Schooling: Educational Anthropology in Action*, edited by G. Spindler, 20–32. New York: Holt Rinehart and Winston.
This chapter describes the difficulties of observing classrooms in the United States that are "familiar" to many educators. The authors compare this "familiar" setting with their anthropological work in "strange" settings and discuss ways of making "familiar" social settings more accessible.

Florio-Ruane, S. 1990. "Creating Your Own Case Studies: A Guide for Early Field Experience." *Teacher Education Quarterly* (Winter): 29–41.
Written for an audience of teachers, teacher educators, and student teachers, this article gives observers ways of looking at classrooms from an ethnographic perspective and considers how events have been constructed overtime.

Flores, S. 1999. "Classrooms as Cultures from a Principal's Perspective." *Primary Voices K–6* 7 (3): 54.
Steve Flores writes about ethnography in education from the perspective of an administrator who observes teachers' classrooms in his own elementary school.

8

Culture and Consciousness

Maria, one of the student teachers wrote a reflection about ethnography:

> A part of me feels that once one has understood the culture of the classroom . . . so what? The transformative process of developing our own cultures is the next step. What kind of environment will I set up? What will be my strengths and weaknesses? How will I develop a classroom culture in which my students feel accountability and responsibility? These are some of the questions I leave with as an ethnographic educator.

In this chapter, I talk about the many changes that took place among the members of our small group and discuss how the combination of ethnography, the teacher education program at our university, and the bilingual elementary school where we did our fieldwork made those changes possible. I begin with my own change of consciousness.

After I began working with these nine student teachers, and after using ethnography in classrooms, I changed in my thinking about the importance of classroom discourse (Cazden 1988). When my principal observed me teaching first grade in the 1980s, he took extensive notes on what I said to my students. I could not understand why he spent so much time writing down the words that I spoke. It was through my experience with ethnography that I was able to understand how our classrooms are created by *the way we speak with our students*. Through conversations teachers and students construct meanings for reading, writing, mathematics, and all other areas of classroom life (Wells and Chang-Wells 1992). Now, when I enter a classroom, I listen to the teacher and students and the words they speak to each other. I also ask my student teachers to do the same. When I talk to the student teachers in my own classroom, I realize the importance of the words we speak together.

Cultural Perspectives

During the year that I worked with these student teachers at Island View Elementary School, I knew very little about other cultural groups. Learning about other cultures and languages changed my own consciousness. I found that I am like the students mentioned in Chapter 4 who enter different classrooms without an understanding of the norms and routines for appropriate participation. As I enter different cultures, I sometimes find myself unable to act because of my inability to read the situation and ask for help. For example, recently I was taking a class on university teaching. In one session, we were asked to do a role-playing activity. This strategy is meant to give students a chance to apply what they are learning. Students are presented with a realistic or hypothetical situation and a cast of characters. The students then improvise dialogue and actions to fit their views of the situation and the character they are playing. In my small group of six, we were given various roles from which to argue our different proposals. I took on the role of a Latino child development major.

One of the first things I thought about was whether or not I could speak with an accent. There were many things to consider. First, the accent that I used would have to have intonation, different vowel sounds, abbreviated words, and slang words that were unique to a bilingual student. I was unsure if I did use an accent, whether or not I would be stereotyping people from the Latino culture. In the moment, I did not have the words I needed to ask questions about this. Now that I reflect back on the event, I realize that I could have pointed out my dilemma to the members of my small group, and we could have discussed it.

Multiple Perspectives

If I am to be successful in changing my consciousness and changing the consciousness of the student teachers I teach, I need to find answers to these kinds of questions. The nine student teachers that I write about in this book experienced many of the same kinds of problems. We were able to discuss these language and cultural differences together during our small group seminars. Aurora described her Neighborhood Walk (see Chapter 2) and how she was opening new paths to viewing her Spanish-speaking students just by seeing where and how they lived. Lydia, Maria, and Ana shared their different Latino cultures. Lydia was born and raised in our same community by parents who immigrated from Mexico. Maria had been raised in Northern California by parents who were part of the Chicano Movement of the 1960s. Ana was a first generation U.S. citizen raised by Argentinian parents. These three showed us the range of differences in both language and culture among Spanish-speaking groups.

Because of these three different Spanish-speaking perspectives, the whole group was learning about particular differences within the Latino community. We could no longer think of Latino culture being all the same (i.e., recent immigrants from Mexico), or all using the same kind of language (i.e., a Chicano accent). In addition, our small group benefited from having two perspectives from Asian cultures. Helen grew up in Southern California in a Japanese American home. Sue was born in Laos and came to the United States with her family when she was five years old.

In our small group seminars, we often discussed our similar and different cultural experiences. We learned how *different* we were because of how we were raised in different cultures even though we were all raised in the United States. But at the same time we also learned how some of our cultural ceremonies were *similar*. For example, in Chapter 2, we discovered that *El Día De Los Muertos* and *Obon* were religious holidays from two different countries that were both meant to honor ancestors. Alice and Aurora also brought to our group a parent perspective, each having sons in public schools. Some of the student teachers had parents who had been teachers for many years, thus broadening our experience with education.

From these diverse perspectives, we examined the culture of the elementary school where the teachers were doing their fieldwork, Island View Elementary School, which was mostly made up of "Hispanic" students. In addition, we learned how to observe from broad perspectives to more focused ones: this community, this family, this school, this classroom, and this student. Through ethnography we learned how to look at details such as how one student would sit on the rug during Calendar Time. At the same time, we learned how to explore the whole community from a broad perspective. Through ethnography we compared one student's actions and talk with another's and compared this neighborhood with other neighborhoods nearby.

In our small group discussions, we developed strategies for talking about the differences between us all and the changes we all went through as we met and interacted with different people. Learning about multiple perspectives gave us all newer ways of observing the world. We began to see that our way of looking at the world was not the only way. In looking from other ways, we expanded our vision and learned how to see from someone else's angle of vision.

A Member's Perspective

Another way that ethnography helped us change our consciousness was through notetaking and notemaking. This strategy, based on a theory of multiple perspectives, helped us all divide our observations of social settings into descriptions and interpretations. By learning how to do this, we discovered that delaying our interpretations enabled us to learn more about the culture from an insiders' perspective. When we did go back and add judgments, interpretations, and evaluations, they were based on evidence built up from taking many notes of the language and actions of the group.

Speaking from evidence instead of personal bias was another way that ethnography was helping to change our consciousness. We could still have our own personal opinions but now we also had different perspectives and biases to consider. We knew that our view was only one of many. In understanding that, we realized that the observations we made always depended on something else. We no longer could say, "This will happen because of that." From our newer consciousness, we had to consider all other points of view and say, "Well, this might happen if that were the case. But if this were the case then this other might happen." In this way we were learning about the complexity of classrooms and how teacher decision making must take into consideration that complexity.

An Overtime Perspective

Realizing that social groups or cultures (or classrooms) form, create, or build routines and patterns of living with each other over time helped us realize that in order to understand how a social group practices everyday life, we had to observe for longer periods of time. If we did not have the time, then we had to at least realize that we could not see or understand everything. We were then infrequent visitors in strange communities with different languages and ways of being, believing, evaluating, and perceiving. If we wanted to observe, we had to take into consideration this inability to see the totality of life in that particular social setting. We learned how to look through an ethnographic perspective (see Chapters 1 and 4), how to become participant observers (see Chapters 2 and 7), how to do ethnographic interviews (see Chapter 3), and how to reflect on our observations (see Chapters 5 and 6).

The ethnographic questions (who can do or say what, when, where, under what conditions, for what purposes and with what outcomes) were helping us ask questions about the implicit, assumed, unacknowledged parts of classroom life. When does the teacher collect the papers? How do students go about sharpening pencils? How do students signal that they have the answer to a math problem? How can students ask questions if they do not understand an assignment? How do students line up for library appropriately? When can students wash their hands for lunch? How do students get the teachers attention? What is really important in this classroom? These ethnographic questions also helped us understand that in each classroom there is an underlying belief system. This system can be seen through the systematic analysis of the cultural language that is built up overtime between teachers and students and is different in every classroom. It is this belief system that takes longer to observe and find. It is also through this belief system that learning is socially created.

A Language Perspective

By learning to listen to the language of the classroom and the way that teachers talked to students, we observed that some of the language of teaching was similar across classrooms. By listening carefully and documenting the language in transcripts, we uncovered principles of practice for teaching (see Chapter 3 on interviews), ways of assessing the progress of our students (see Chapter 5 on case studies), and ways that we could change our own teaching (see Chapter 6 on reflection). By making the language concrete, something we could see and touch, we saw how we could change it. Or, we were able to name and identify the strategies that we used. By doing this we could point out, to ourselves and to others, the kind of things we did as teachers, why we did them, what they were for, and how they helped (or hindered) students in the classroom.

A Teaching Perspective

Some teachers are using ethnography to construct a language and a method for describing what we do in classrooms (see the January 1999 issue of *Primary Voices K–6*; see also Egan-Robertson and Bloome [1998]). It is possible to systematically and effectively explain our practice to others through ethnography. Ethnographers engage in participant observation in order to learn the language and ways of the members of a culture. They explain and describe the "emic" (or insider) perspective. In order to write an ethnography, an account that describes the culture, the ethnographer must *translate* that information back into outsider (or "etic") language. Teachers can use ethnography for just that purpose. We can describe to outsiders what we know about classrooms through ethnography. As Sue said in Chapter 3, "Learning to teacher talk is for me like learning a new language." That is because it *is* a different language. All cultures have different ways of speaking, different cover terms and names for things, and different ways of evaluating and believing. Through ethnography teachers can help outsiders understand the culture of teaching.

In addition, ethnography can improve our teaching practice. By using ethnography to reflect on what we do as teachers in classrooms, we can examine and analyze the instructional strategies we use and discover the reasons why we use them. In this way we can make visible the links between theory and practice. By slowing down the language and action of the classroom, with videotapes, audiotapes, and transcriptions, we can put what we do into concrete terms. We can chart our events and catalog our language to systematically examine practice from an insider perspective. As a group, we can use our professional language to observe learning in the classroom and explain this learning to ourselves, to our colleagues, to our newest members, to policymakers, and to parents.

A Learning Perspective

Knowing how to see and understand our own culture will help us learn how to see others. If we use ethnography to uncover, examine, describe, and explain our own perspective on teaching and learning in classrooms, then we can use it in other situations to learn about other ways of being. We will become lifelong observers of culture, lifelong learners, and change our consciousness, not only as teachers and students but as people.

Afterword
Being Part of Everyone Else

At the end of this school year, the nine student teachers went their separate ways. This book brought us back together for a few moments and we are grateful for that. These teachers are now using their knowledge of ethnography in their own classrooms. Maria, Josh, and Mary have gone to the Bay Area to teach. Helen will soon join them after teaching in Los Angeles. Sue was teaching in a kindergarten in Los Angeles this past year. Aurora, Alice, and Lydia stayed in the same city where we did our study. Aurora taught sixth graders, Alice worked with gifted students, and Lydia was in a bilingual class. Ana went south to Orange County to work in a two-way bilingual classroom.

I wondered what kinds of classroom communities these nine student teachers created in their own situations and I hoped that ethnography had helped them in realizing that the kind of culture that is formed in classrooms determines the kind of learning that takes place. As I looked over the journals one last time, I found a reflection by Mary that encouraged me. Mary was writing in the spring about entering her second placement and discussed all the different ways that her cooperating teacher had welcomed her into the room and made her feel like part of the group.

> It has been quite a jump to go from first to fourth grade for my placement, although I am definitely getting used to the change. [My cooperating teacher] runs her classroom the way I would like to when I begin teaching! At first it was a little overwhelming to come into a classroom in the middle of the year and feel like I knew nothing about what these students were used to or expected. However, I was so welcomed into this community (and that is exactly what it is) by all of the students and [my cooperating teacher]. I received letters from each of the students about what they liked

about their class and some of the things they do each day. There was also a bulletin board for me in which each student drew a picture of themselves and welcomed me into their classroom with a short note. On the first day I was there full time, the students were able to "interview" me and ask questions to get to know a little bit about me that they may have been wondering during their morning meeting. Some of the questions they asked were so funny! [My cooperating teacher] and I have also been keeping a two-way journal almost daily. This has helped me so much already. She asked me what my expectations of her were as a cooperating teacher, and she told me what she expected of me.

When I asked Mary what the students had asked her, she wrote:

> On my first day in the classroom during the morning meeting, the students were able to ask me any questions they wanted in order to find out a little more about me. All they knew about me was that I was a student teacher and I was going to be taking Josh's place. They were full of questions and most of them were so funny. They began with questions about my family, age, if I had a boyfriend, if Josh was my boyfriend, and they moved to what was my favorite food (when I said pizza, they were ecstatic—it's a very popular food in fourth grade), my favorite color, sea animal, land animal, if I liked rainbows, horses, unicorns, etc. It was very easy for me to see what types of things were important to them. I was able to learn about them through the letters they had written me. I really think this played a big part in me immediately becoming a member of the classroom community. The entire class (my cooperating teacher and all the students) have been sharing and including me in their classroom culture since the first day so I have never really felt like an outsider.

As I read over this journal, I thought about other students in other classrooms who could become members in the same way as this student teacher. By thinking of our classrooms as cultures, we can welcome newcomers in ways that make them feel part of the community instead of outsiders. I remembered what another student, a sixth-grader, had written about becoming a member of his class:

> Our community has a lot to do over the year. Sometimes our community gets different during the year. What I mean is like the first day I walked in the door, I was new and nervous, just me thinking who am I, trying to make friends. I came in the door. Other students explained how to do the Writer's Workshop. I didn't understand the three logs. Other kids and the teacher explained. Now I'm just part of everyone else. (Green and Dixon 1993, 235)

Work Cited

Green, J. L., and C. N. Dixon. 1993. "Talking Knowledge into Being: Discursive and Social Practices in Classrooms." *Linguistics and Education* 5 (3 & 4): 231–39.

References

Agar, M. 1994. *Language Shock: Understanding the Culture of Conversation.* New York: William Morrow.

———. 1980. *The Professional Stranger: An Informal Introduction to Ethnography.* New York: Academic Press.

Atkinson, P. 1990. *The Ethnographic Imagination: Textual Constructions of Reality.* London: Routledge.

Barr, M., D. Craig, D. Fisette, and M. Syverson. 1999. *Assessing Literacy with the Learning Record: Handbook for K–6.* Portsmouth, NH: Heinemann.

Bloome, D. 1985. "Reading as a Social Process." *Language Arts* 62 (2): 134–42.

Brandts, L. R. 1999. "Are Pullout Programs Sabotaging Classroom Community in Our Elementary Schools?" *Primary Voices K–6* (January): 9–16.

———. Personal Communication. (Spring 1997). Email message.

Carini, P. F. 1986. "Building from Children's Strengths." *Journal of Education* 168 (3): 13–24.

Cazden, C. 1988. *Classroom Discourse: The Language of Teaching and Learning.* Portsmouth, NH: Heinemann.

Charney, R. S. 1993. *Teaching Children to Care: Management in the Responsive Classroom.* Greenfield, MA: Northeast Foundation for Children.

Clifford, J. 1986. Introduction: Partial Truths. In *Writing Culture: The Poetics and Politics of Ethnography,* edited by J. Clifford and G. E. Marcus, 1–26. Berkeley: University of California Press.

Collins, E., and J. L. Green. 1992. "Learning in Classroom Settings: Making or Breaking a Culture." In *Redefining Learning: Roots of Educational Restructuring,* edited by H. Marshall, 59–86. Norwood, NJ: Ablex.

Craviotto, E., A. I. Heras, and J. Espíndola. 1999. "Cultures of the Fourth-Grade Bilingual Classroom." *Primary Voices K–6* (January): 25–36.

Cruse, A. 1995. "Unraveling the Sequence: Micro Reflection on Literacy Practices, A Case Study." Presentation at National Reading Conference, December 1997.

Dewey, J. 1986 [1933]. "How We Think: A Restatement of the Relation of Reflective Thinking to the Educative Process." In *John Dewey: The Later Works, 1925–1953, Vol. 8,* edited by J. A. Boydston, 105–352. Carbondale, IL: Southern Illinois University Press.

Dixon, C. N., C. R. Frank, and J. L. Green. 1999. "Classrooms as Cultures: Toward Understanding the Constructed Nature of Life in Classrooms." *Primary Voices K–6* 7 (3): 4–8.

Dixon, C., and H. Horn. 1995. "Writing Across the Curriculum." In *School Improvement Programs,* edited by J. Block, C. Everson, and Guskely, 247–64.

Doyle, J. 1972. "Helpers, Officers, and Lunchers: Ethnography of a Third-Grade Class." In *The Cultural Experience: Ethnography in Complex Society,* edited by J. Spradley and D. McCurdy, 147–56. Prospect Heights, IL: Waveland Press.

Dyson, A. H. 1995. "Children out of Bounds: The Power of Case Studies in Expanding Visions of Literacy Development." In *A Handbook for Literacy Educators: Research on Teaching the Communicative and Visual Arts,* edited by J. Flood, S. B. Heath, and D. Lapp. New York: Macmillan.

———. 1993. *Social Worlds of Children Learning to Write in an Urban Primary School.* New York: Teachers College Press.

Egan-Robertson, A., and D. Bloome, eds. 1998. *Students as Researchers of Culture and Language in Their Own Communities.* Cresskill, NJ: Hampton Press.

Erickson, F. 1982. "Classroom Discourse as Improvisation: Relationships Between Academic Task Structure and Social Participation in Lessons." In *Communicating in the Classroom,* edited by L. C. Wilkinson, 153–82. New York: Academic Press.

Evertson, C., and J. L. Green. 1986. "Observation as Inquiry and Method." In *Handbook of Research on Teaching,* 3d ed., edited by M. C. Wittrock. New York: Macmillan.

Firestone, W. A. 1992. "Organizational Design and Teaching for Student Learning." In *Redefining Student Learning: Roots of Educational Change,* edited by H. H. Marshall, 265–91. Norwood, NJ: Ablex.

Florio-Ruane, S. 1990. "Creating Your Own Case Studies: A Guide for Early Field Experience." *Teacher Education Quarterly* (Winter): 29–41.

Frank, C. R. 1997. *The Children Who Owned All the Words in the World: An Ethnography of Writing Workshop in Second Grade.* Ph.D. diss., University of California, Santa Barbara.

Frank, C. R., C. N. Dixon, and L. R. Brandts. 1998. "'Dear Book Club': A Sociolinguistic and Ethnographic Analysis of Literature Discussion Groups in Second Grade." In *Forty-Seventh National Reading Conference Yearbook,* edited by T. Shanahan and F. Rodriguez-Brown. NRC.

Graves, D. H. 1983. *Writing: Teachers and Children at Work.* Exeter, NH: Heinemann.

Green, J. L. 1992. "Multiple Perspectives: Issues and Directions. In *Multidisciplinary Perspectives on Literacy Research,* edited by R. Beach, J. L. Green, M. L. Kamil, and T. Shanahan. Urbana, IL: NCTE.

———. 1983. "Research on Teaching as a Linguistic Process: A State of the Art. *Review of Research in Education,* 10:152–252.

Green, J. L., and C. N. Dixon. 1999. Ethnographic interview at the University of California, Santa Barbara, on February 20–21.

———. 1993. "Talking Knowledge into Being: Discursive and Social Practices in Classrooms." *Linguistics and Education* 5 (3/4): 231–39.

Green, J. L., and C. Wallat. 1981. "Mapping Instructional Conversations: A Sociolinguistic Ethnography." In *Ethnography and Language in Educational Settings,* edited by J. L. Green and C. Wallat, 161–205. Norwood, NJ: Ablex.

Green, J. L., and D. Bloome. 1997. "Ethnography and Ethnographers of and in Education: A Situated Perspective." In *Handbook for Research in the Communicative and Visual Arts,* edited by S. B. Heath, J. Flood, and D. Lapp, 181–202. New York: Macmillan.

Hayano, D. M. 1978. "Strategies for the Management of Luck and Action in an Urban Poker Parlor." *Urban Life and Culture* 6: 475–88.

Heap, J. 1980. "What Counts as Reading? Limits to Certainty in Assessment." *Curriculum Inquiry* 10 (3): 265–92.

Heath, S. B. 1983. *Ways with Words: Language, Life and Work in Communities and Classrooms.* Cambridge: Cambridge University Press.

Jennings, L. 1998. "Reading the World of the Classroom Through Ethnographic Eyes." *The California Reader* 31 (4): 11–15.

Jones, E., and E. Prescott. 1978. *Dimensions of Teaching–Learning Environments.* Pasadena, CA: Pacific Oaks College.

Kanevsky, R. 1993. "Descriptive Review of a Child: A Way of Knowing About Teaching and Learning." In *Inside–Outside: Teacher Research and Knowledge,* edited by M. Cochran-Smith and S. Lytle. New York: Teachers College Press.

Lin, L. 1993. "Language of and in the Classroom: Constructing the Patterns of Social Life." *Linguistics and Education* 5: 367–409.

Lutz, F. W. 1981. "Ethnography: The Holistic Approach to Understanding Schooling." In *Ethnography and Language in Educational Settings,* edited by J. Green and C. Wallat. Norwood, NJ: Ablex.

Marshall, H. H. 1992. "Seeing, Redefining, and Supporting Student Learning." In *Redefining Student Learning: Roots of Educational Change,* edited by H. H. Marshall, 1–32. Norwood, NJ: Ablex.

McCarthey, S. J. 1997. "Connecting Home and School Literacy Practices in Classrooms with Diverse Populations." *Journal of Literacy Research* 29 (2): 145–82.

Mehan, H. 1979. *Learning Lessons: Social Organization in the Classroom.* Cambridge, MA: Harvard University.

Popper, K. 1963. *Conjectures and Refutations.* London: Routledge & Kegan Paul.

Putney, L. A. 1997. Historicity in Action: An Ethnographic Study of Collective/Individual Discourse in a Fifth-Grade Bilingual Class. Ph.D. diss., University of California, Santa Barbara.

Robertson, S. 1996. Dialectical Journals. In *Into Focus: Understanding and Creating Middle School Readers,* edited by G. K. Beers and B. G. Samuels.

Santa Barbara Classroom Discourse Group. 1992a. "Constructing Literacy in Classrooms: Literate Action as Social Accomplishment." In *Redefining Student*

Learning: Roots of Educational Change, edited by H. H. Marshall, 119–50. Norwood, NJ: Ablex.

———. 1992b. "Do You See What We See? The Referential and Intertextual Nature of Classroom Life." *Journal of Classroom Interaction* 27 (2): 29–36.

Sendak, M. 1962. *Chicken Soup with Rice.* New York: Harper & Row.

Spindler, G., and L. Spindler. 1982. "Roger Harker and Schonhausen: From Familiar to Strange and Back Again." In *Doing the Ethnography of Schooling: Educational Anthropology in Action,* edited by G. Spindler, 20–32. New York: Holt Rinehart & Winston.

Spradley, J. P. 1980. *Participant Observation.* San Francisco: Holt, Rinehart & Winston.

———. 1979. *The Ethnographic Interview.* New York: Harcourt Brace Jovanovich.

———. 1972. *Culture and Cognition: Rules, Maps, and Plans.* San Francisco: Chandler.

Spradley, J. P., and D. W. McCurdy. 1972. *The Cultural Experience: Ethnography in Complex Society.* Prospect Heights, IL: Waveland Press.

Stauffer, R. G. 1975. *Directing the Reading-Thinking Process.* New York: Harper & Row.

Sulzby, E. 1985. Kindergartners as Readers and Writers. In *Advances in Writing Research Vol. 1: Children's Early Writing Development,* edited by M. Farr, 127–99. Norwood, NJ: Ablex.

Sunstein, B. S., and Green M. 1994. *Composing a Culture: Inside a Summer Writing Program for High School Teachers.* Portsmouth, NH: Boynton/Cook.

Tuyay, S. 1999. "Our Trip to Space." *Primary Voices K–6* (January): 17–24.

Valdés, G. 1996. *Con Respeto: Bridging the Distances Between Culturally Diverse Families and Schools: An Ethnographic Portrait.* New York: Teachers College Press.

Wallat, C., J. L. Green, S. Conlin, and M. Haramis. 1983. "Issues Related to Action Research in the Classroom: The Teacher and Researcher as a Team." In *Ethnography and Language in Educational Settings,* edited by J. L. Green and C. Wallat, 87–113. Norwood, NJ: Ablex.

Wells, G., and G. L. Chang-Wells. 1992. *Constructing Knowledge Together.* Portsmouth, NH: Heinemann.

Yeager, B. 1999. "Constructing a Community of Inquirers." *Primary Voices K–6* (January): 37–52.

Yeager, B., A. Floriani, and J. Green. 1998. Learning to See Learning in the Classroom: Developing an Ethnographic Perspective. In *Students as Researchers of Culture and Language in Their Own Communities,* edited by A. Egan-Robertson and D. Bloome, 115–40. Cresskill, NJ: Hampton Press.

Bottom row: Lourdes Monarres, Joe Hedgecock
Middle row: Dawn Burns, Heidi Kubota, Malín Ramírez, Adriana Lopez
Top row: Samantha Xaymountry, Carolyn Frank, Carmen Allison, Monica Savena

Index